How To Cr Amigurumi For Beginners

Abbyr .T Richmondn

Health Advantages of Crochet

I'm addicted to yarn. I'm not joking; I genuinely enjoy handling, feeling, and admiring yarn. Simply put, it brings me great joy. The best part is that working with yarn has many positive health effects and is not a bad addiction.

The wonderful activity of crocheting has many advantages for both the body and the mind. Crafting with yarn has existed for centuries. The first known art form, weaving has been around for 30,000 years.

The advantages of knitting with yarn have thus been the subject of numerous studies because they have endured for such a long time.

OWL IN CROCHET HERE

While I primarily crochet, I also latch hook and am beginning to learn how to weave. Because of this, I believe it's crucial that you understand how beneficial all forms of yarn craft—including knitting, weaving, latch hooking, embodiery, etc.—can be.

Just in case you need more justification for enjoying working with those heavenly strands. Let's begin!

DECREASED ANXIETY

The body's natural reaction to stress is anxiety, but for some people, it occurs far too frequently. Having something enjoyable to do can save your life. Since crocheting has the ability to calm your body, mind, and spirit with just a few stitches, it can be very beneficial in this regard. A person with high levels of anxiety may be too stressed to begin meditating, so it can be very helpful for them to meditate while crocheting.

SUBSTANCES DEPRESSION

Crocheting has been known to help pull people out of chronic depression or at the very least get them through a terrible, brief trip down depression lane. There are many curveballs that life throws your way.

Therefore, having a constant in your life that you can manage, build upon, and gain experience from can bring you a truly magical sense of peace and happiness. It's a creative outlet that can assist you in positively exploring and expressing your emotions.

Due to its self-generated nature and flexibility, this kind of happiness is crucial in the face of depression.

BUILDING SELF-ESTEEM

In addition to giving you a sense of control, crocheting can make you feel accomplished. You can look at all the rows or projects that you completed and know that you did this when you finish a project, no matter how big or small, or when you're feeling unproductive.

You also gain the advantage of developing a permanent skill. People have been able to pick up crocheting again after a brief refresher even after taking extended breaks.

Crocheting is one of the skills in which I personally feel the most comfortable. It can really help you get through a lot of things to feel confident in something.

LOWERS STRESS

Stress has the potential to kill. It can result in a variety of health issues and is one of the main causes of disease (get it? dis-ease). Crocheting or knitting is a great way to relax because it gives your brain something to focus on without having to think about it too much.

It's a convenient, simple method for assisting your brain in letting go of stress, and if you don't have much time, you can choose a small project that you can complete in a restroom stall if necessary! Simply keep a small ball of yarn and a hook with you at all times in your bag, pocket, or vehicle.

Try my crocheted hearts if you're looking for a simple, quick pattern; they only take 3-5 minutes to complete and will help you de-stress.

RENDERS AND ELIMINATES DEMENTIA

Numerous studies have shown that knitting and crocheting not only provide comfort to those who are suffering from dementia but also delay the onset of age-related memory loss. Mild cognitive impairment, which is thought to be an early sign of dementia, was found to be reduced by 30% to 50% in elderly people who started knitting, reading, and playing games. Additionally, it helped people with more severe memory loss.

ASSISTS IN GRIEF

Everybody goes through grief at some point; whether it involves a human or a furry loved one, it's a trying time for the survivors. By giving your hands something to do, crocheting can temporarily distract you from your sorrow and grief while also improving your mood. All wounds will eventually heal with time, but crocheting has the power to speed up the process. Grief frequently causes depression, anxiety, and stress, so the fact that crocheting has been shown to help with all of these symptoms is very beneficial for the practitioner.

RELIGION FOR AIDS

Whatever your religion or political stance, prayer is a spiritual practice. It has long been acknowledged to contain the power of faith, which is said to be capable of moving mountains. Being quite spiritual, crocheting for me is the same as making something with my own two hands. When done with intention and purpose, crocheting is a form of spirituality. There are a lot of people who crochet prayer shawls and blankets for loved ones and charities, so it seems like I'm not the only one who feels that way.

I invite you to try crocheting something with good

intentions for someone you care about, even if you're not particularly spiritual. Choose a repetitive pattern, and as you crochet, consider that person. Consider their strengths and the things you want the best for them. Just give it a try and see how it feels, even if it's for your pet.

HELP FOR INSISTENCY

We've all been there: lying in bed late at night, staring up at the ceiling, hoping to fall asleep before dawn. You simply think about too many things, have errands to run, conversations to have, and embarrassing things to remember saying ten years ago...

Crocheting before bed can help your mind unwind and relax enough to allow you to feel sleepy, and the act of concentrating on one thing can help you fall asleep more quickly. It doesn't have to be this way, though.

FOCUS ON AIDS

Focusing, by which I mean, man, can you veer off course! You are cleaning something one moment, and the next you are considering your entry into this room. Is that a squirrel over there? Brain fog is a real thing, and it can be extremely frustrating. Could you repeat that, please? I had in mind a location on the wall just behind you.

It's unpleasant and is brought on by hormonal imbalances brought on by stress and occasionally a disorganized mind. The best way to aid in brain reorganization is to actively immerse yourself in something, pay attention to every detail, and maintain your lovely mind on the tasks at hand. Basically, practice being mindful. By mindfully meditating while crocheting, you can achieve this. By teaching your brain to focus on one thing, you are demonstrating to it how to do it on other things. Your brain loves to look for patterns and compare one thing to another.

DELIVERS A SENSE OF CONTROL

The world is how you see it where you are spinning your yarn. You choose the projects, the yarn weight, the colors, the patterns, the stitches, and the hook sizes. All of this is up to you, and knowing that can help you feel much more at ease and in control in a world where you might otherwise feel powerless.

AID FOR ADDICTION

Due to its addictive nature, crocheting has actually

been used in rehabilitation facilities to help patients overcome their addictions by substituting knitting or crocheting for their current unhealthy addiction.

It keeps your hands and mind occupied and can aid in tremor control through concentration. Usually, you'll want to continue working on a project once you start crocheting it. You may be able to successfully break your eating, drinking, and drug-using habits thanks to this.

AID FOR MEDITATION

Meditation's health benefits have been the subject of so many studies that I believe everyone is now aware of it. Yarn craft can help because for some people, it's easier said than done.

It's incredibly simple to meditate while knitting or crocheting; all you have to do is immerse yourself in your natural breathing pattern, hand motions, and rhythm. the texture of the yarn and the appearance of the color.

Use both hands equally when crocheting, paying attention to the texture of the fabric you're producing with your hands. Make sure to actively feed your yarn onto your hook, avoid having stiff hands, and let the motion and your breathing work as a single unit.

AID FOR FINER MOTOR SKILLS

Many people have discovered that fiber arts, such as crocheting, have helped them regain or improve their fine motor skills.

Even now, there is a push to get kids to learn how to knit or crochet so that their fine motor skills can advance faster and in a more enjoyable way.

All of these advantages point to the fact that crocheting, as well as knitting, latch hooking, making pom-poms, and other related crafts, doubles as an excellent form of self care.

I hope you've discovered the advantages of crocheting in your own life. Anyone and everyone can benefit from this wonderful yarny habit.

Contents

CHAPTER 1 - BASIC STITCHES

This is designed to give you some of the most basic crochet stitches that are very beginner-friendly. You can use these stitches for entire projects or the basis of these stitches as a frame for more advanced stitches found later in this guide.

Single Crochet

When learning how to crochet, single crochet will become your best friend. It is the core stitch you will need to learn because it is incorporated into many crochet patterns you will come across.

The single crochet has the appearance of a very tight piece of fabric. It has very few holes in it and has distinctive uniform rows that look elegant and crisp. This gives your work a very clean look.

Heightwise, single crochet is one of the smallest of the crochet stitches; therefore, work tends to build slowly when using this stitch.

To single crochet begin with your chain or row, insert your crochet hook into the next stitch or chain along. Put your yarn over your hook and draw that yarn through the hole, once you have brought the yarn through the stitch or chain you should now have 2 loops on your hook.

Yarn over again and draw that yarn through both of these loops on your hook. You should now be left with only 1 loop on your hook, and that is it! That is how simple single crochet is.

Slip Stitch

A slip stitch, like the single crochet, is one of the basics. It has a huge variety of uses and is crucial to learn early. A row of slip stitches looks very uniform and tight. This stitch is not typically used for large sheets of fabric or objects due to how tightness of the stitches.

The most common use for this stitch is for crossing a row without adding any more height to your work. It is also used to make something tighter, such as the rim of a hat. Slip stitches are commonly used to join two bits of work together, such as two sheets of fabric; to do this you work a slip stitch through both pieces of fabric to join them together.

To slip stitch insert your crochet hook into the next stitch along, yarn over and draw this yarn from back to front through the stitch, now bring that yarn through the loop that is already on your hook, and that is it! This can be a little fiddly to get the hang of, but you can make it easier by making the loop on your hook a little looser, this helps with pulling the yarn through the loop.

Double Crochet

Double crochet is twice the height of a single crochet and is just as easy. This crochet stitch has a much more open look and projects using this stitch will build very quickly. Due to the height of this stitch, you will tend to need a larger starting chain; otherwise, your work can begin to look warped.

To double crochet, begin by yarning over your hook, this will leave you with 2 loops on your hook. Insert the crochet hook into the next stitch (or 3rd stitch if starting at the beginning of a row) and yarn over once more and draw that yarn through the stitch. You will now have 3 loops on your hook. Yarn over once again and draw that yarn through 2 of the 3 loops only, once this is complete you will have 2 loops left on the hook. Yarn over a final time and draw the yarn through the last 2 loops on your hook and you are done.

Half Double Crochet

This stitch is a variant of a double crochet. The height of this stitch is the hallway between single and double crochet. This stitch has fewer steps than double crochet which makes it a favorite among many people. Another significant attribute of this stitch is that it is tall like a double crochet but has the density of a single crochet.

To make a half double crochet, begin by yarning over your hook. This will leave you with 2 loops on your hook. Insert the crochet hook into the next stitch and yarn over once more and draw that yarn through the stitch, you will now have 3 loops on your hook. At this point, all of these steps are the same as double crochet, it is how you finish the stitch that is different. Yarn over and pull that yarn through all 3 loops that are on your hook to complete the stitch, and that is it!

Treble Crochet

A treble crochet is a very tall stitch. It is commonly used for large open projects such as lightweight blankets. This stitch does require quite a few steps, but once you have mastered how to do this, it will not take very long at all. As with double crochet, you will need to compensate when turning your work by chaining 3-5 depending on the pattern.

To begin yarn over 2 times, you should start with 3 loops on your hook. Insert your hook into the stitch, yarn over and pull the yarn through the stitch giving you 4 loops on the hook. Yarn over and pull through 2 of the 4 loops on your hook, you will be left with 3 loops after pulling through. Yarn over again and pull through another 2 loops; you will be left with 2 loops on your hook. Yarn over a final time and pull through the remaining 2 loops on your hook. Yes, it is a bit time-consuming and tricky to work with, but the results are worth it.

A great way to remember how many times to pull through the loops is in the names, a single crochet only pulls through the loops once; a double crochet pulls through the loops twice, and the treble crochet will pull through the loops three times.

Front Post Double Crochet

The front post double crochet can be tricky to learn, especially if you are new to crochet. The confusion comes from the placement of your hook. The front post double crochet is simply a regular double crochet, but what makes it unique is where you will place your hook before beginning this stitch.

The finished stitch will give you the effect of a raised edge or ridge through your work. When used in conjunction with a back post double crochet, it can create a beautiful pattern.
To begin do a standard row of double crochet, this is your foundation for this stitch. If the foundation is not done, the stitch will not work. Chain 2 when you reach the end of this row.

At the beginning of your new row, yarn over and instead of inserting your hook into the top of the double crochet stitch, go under and around the stitch or post itself as shown.
Now yarn over and pull the yarn through the way you came. Finish off with a regular double crochet by yarning over and going through 2 loops, yarning over and going through the final 2 loops.

Back Post-Double Crochet

Like the front post double crochet, this is simply a glorified double crochet, but put into a different place to create a unique little design in your work. This stitch can be used by itself or in conjunction with the front post double crochet to create a fun raised and sunken texture within your projects.

To begin, do a regular row of double crochet to form the foundation for this stitch Chain 2 at the end of your row for turning.
Now yarn over and instead of going into the top of the stitch, go behind your work and insert your hook around the post of the stitch as shown.

From this position, yarn over and pull the yarn through the path through which you came to draw up a loop. Once you have your 3 loops on the hook, yarn over and draw through 2 loops. Yarn over and pull through the final 2 loops just like in a regular double crochet. The front and back post double crochet work very well together and can create a type of stitch known as a basket weave, covered later on in this guide. These two stitches are also a perfect example of how you can take a regular basic stitch like the double crochet and alter it slightly to give you a great effect.

Front Loop Crochet

Not to be confused with the similar front post crochet, this stitch is simple and doesn't have much of an impact. The stitch can make your plain objects have a touch of pizazz with no extra effort; as it utilizes a very basic and user-friendly single crochet.

To begin, first, you need to see where your crochet hook goes. You can see from the top view of a chain or row of single crochet that you have two distinctive loops. For a regular crochet, you would use both of these loops when inserting your hook, however, for a front loop crochet, you will be going through that first loop closest to you only!

Once at this stage simply yarn over and pull through. Yarn over and go through both 2 loops on your hook exactly as you would in a double crochet, there is nothing more to this stitch, but to make more of them!

Back Loop Crochet

Just like in the front loop crochet, do not get this stitch confused with a back post double crochet as they are 2 different things. Just like the front loop crochet, this stitch utilizes the basic single crochet to create a pattern that is unique. This particular type of crochet is also used in making items like shoes and containers, as it manipulates the yarn to bend and fold in the required directions.

To begin, you need to see where your crochet hook goes, you can clearly see from the top view of a chain or row of single crochet that you have two distinctive loops.

For a regular crochet, you would use both of these loops when inserting your hook. However, for a back loop crochet, you will be inserting your hook through the back loop only. Once you have done this, yarn over as you would with a single crochet, pull the yarn through, yarn over and pull through both of the 2 loops on your hook to complete the stitch.

Moss Stitch

The Moss stitch uses 2 different crochet stitches to add a unique look to your work. This is a simple yet intriguing stitch that will spruce up many of your projects. Begin at the beginning of your row, and start by putting a regular half double crochet in that first stitch, and then slip stitch into the next stitch. Repeat this pattern of one-half double crochet and one slip stitch to the end of the row. You will be able to clearly see a little dip in your work wherever you did a slip stitch.

Once you reach the end of your row, chain 1 and turn your work. Now on this row, you want to do the complete opposite of the earlier row, this means wherever you put a half-double crochet you now want to do a slip stitch, and wherever there is a slip stitch you want to do a half double crochet.

If you forget what stitch is where, you can look at the stitch below it. If the bottom stitch is smaller than the next stitch, then it was a slip stitch, if it's higher than the next stitch, then it was a half double crochet. Keep working on this pattern until you are happy with the length of your work.

Basket Stitch

It uses both the front and back post double crochet, but in a particular pattern to create a beautiful texture to any pattern. This type of stitch is mainly used for table runners, hats and blankets. The reason is that the stitch takes a long time to complete, and the result is a dense fabric. However, you can experiment with using this stitch in any project you would like.

First, start off with the correct number of chains because this pattern relies on multiples. This means you must always have enough chains in that multiple. For example, if you decide that you want 4 stitches per basket stitch then your overall number of chains should be a multiple of 4, such as 16. If you wanted 5 stitches, then it would be a multiple of 5, such as 20. For this demonstration, we will be using a multiple of 4.

Begin by having a chain of 16 with an extra 2 for your stitch allowance. Next put one double crochet in each stitch to the end of the row, chain 2 and turn your work. At this stage, you now want to do 4 back post double crochets, and then 4 front post double crochets, repeat this pattern to complete the row, chain 2 and turn.

Now repeat the pattern but this time in reverse. So, wherever you put a front post double crochet, put a back post double crochet and vice versa. Simply repeat this pattern till your work is at a length you are happy with.

X Stitch

The X stitch is a very open type of stitch.
Note: this particular stitch requires knowledge of the double crochet.

This stitch is worked over 2 stitches. Be sure your chain or row is an even number so you can fit all the stitches.
To begin, skip the first stitch and put a double crochet into the second stitch. Once you complete the first double crochet, yarn over and insert the hook into the stitch or chain that you skipped earlier.

Complete this by going around the back of the first stitch, into the stitch, yarn over and pull through before finishing off as a regular double crochet.

This stitch is a little tricky to get your head around in the beginning, but it is well worth the effort as you can add a unique look to your work.

CHAPTER 2 - AMIGURUMI PATTERNS

Jerry the Koala

Required: 20 g of light grey acrylic, 1-2 grams of white or off-white yarn for the ears and 2 g of black yarn for the nose (I used BERNAT Premium), H hook (5 mm), a pair of 10 mm safety eyes, tapestry needle, polyester stuffing.

This toy consists of the head, body, 4 legs, 2 ears and a nose.

Head

Rnd 1. with grey yarn: 6 sc into MR (6)
Rnd 2. 6 inc (12)
Rnd 3. (sc, inc) x 6 times (18)
Rnd 4. (2 sc, inc) x 6 times (24)
Rnd 5. (3 sc, inc) x 6 times (30)
Rnd 6-10. (30)
Rnd 11. (3 sc, dec) x 6 times (24)
Rnd 12. (2 sc, dec) x 6 times (18). Begin stuffing. Insert a pair
of safety eyes at round Rnd 10-11 with 8-9 stitches apart.
Rnd 13. (1 sc, dec) x 6 times (12). Add some stuffing if needed.
Rnd 14. 6 dec.
Fasten off and cut the yarn with enough length to sew it later.

Body

Rnd 1. with grey yarn: 6 sc into MR (6)
Rnd 2. 6 inc (12)
Rnd 3. (sc, inc) x 6 times (18)
Rnd 4. 18 sc in BLO
Rnd 5-12. 18 sc, Stuff as you ga
Rnd 13. (1 sc, dec) x 6 times (12). Add some stuffing to make it firm.
Fasten off and cut the yarn with enough length to sew it later.

Ears (make 2)

With white or beige yarn make 6 sc in MR, don't connect it in a circle, just turn and work from the other side to get a half-circle.

Change color to the main grey and work 6 inc (12). Fasten off and cut the yarn with enough on the end to sew it later. I usually make a double knot of 2 ends at the color-changing point and cut both ends. One more end (white) is left from the MR, I weave and cut it too (see the right ear with the weaved end before I cut it). You should end up with only 1 end of the main color for sewing (see the next picture).

Legs (make 4)

Rnd 1. with grey yarn: 4 sc into MR (4)
Rnd 2. Inc in every stitch (8)
Rnd 3. 8 sc in BLO
Rnd 4-7. 8 sc
Fasten off and cut the yarn with enough length to sew it. Stuff the details loosely

Nose (black)

With black color make 3 sc in MR, don't connect it in a circle, just turn and work from the other side to get a half-circle as for the ears.
Rnd 2. 3 sc, turn
Rnd 3. Inc, sc, inc (5). Fasten off and leave the end for sewing to the face.

Assembling

Sew the ears and the nose to the face as shown in the picture. Attach the head to the body and all 4 limbs symmetrically, see the picture on the right showing the correct placement of the leg (view from the bottom of the toy).

Yay, your koala bear is done!

Fred the Rabbit

Fred is such an adorable little bunny that you would love to keep around the house. With perfect long ears, he is a unique gift for everyone. You can make Fred colorful, too. Just run wild with your imagination and you could have a whole family of bunnies ready to play with.

What You Need:

- DK/ worsted yarn in the color of your choice
- 4 mm crochet hook
- A pair of 6 mm safety eyes

Stuffing

Embroidery needle to sew

Head & Body
R1: 6 sc in MR (6)
R2: inc in each st (12)
R3: (sc 1, inc 1) *6 (18)
R4: (sc 2, inc 1) *6 (24)
R5: (sc 3, inc 1) *6 (30)
R6: (sc 4, inc 1) *6 (36)
R7: (sc 5, inc 1) *6 (42)
R8–14: sc in each st (42)
Attach safety eyes at R11.
R15: (sc 5, dec 1) *6 (36)
R16: (sc 4, dec 1) *6 (30)
R17: (sc 3, dec 1) *6 (24)
R18: (sc 2, dec 1) *6 (18)
R19: (sc 1, dec 1) * 6 (12)
Stuff the head and continue working the body.
R20: (sc 5, inc 1) * 2 (14)
R21: (sc 1, inc 1) * 7 (21)
R22: (sc 2, inc 1) * 7 (28)
R23–28: sc in each st (28)
R29: (sc 2, dec 1) *7 (21)
R30: (sc 1, dec 1) *7 (14)
R31: dec * 7 (7)
Stuff the body well.
Fasten off and weave in the ends.

Ears (Make 2)

R1: 5 sc in MR (5)
R2: inc in each st (10)
R3: (sc 1, inc 1) * 5 (15)
R4–5: sc in each st (15)
R6: (sc 3, dec 1) * 3 (12)
R7: sc in each st (12)
R8: (sc 2, dec 1) * 3 (9)
R9: sc in each st (9)
R10: (sc 1, dec 1) *3 (6)
FO leaving a long tail to sew.
Sew the ears to the top of the head.

Arms (Make 2)

R1: 6 sc in MR (6)
R2: (sc 1, inc 1) * 3 (9)
R3: sc in each st (9)
R4: (sc 1, dec 1) * 3 (6)
R5–8: sc in each st
FO leaving a long tail to sew.
Attach the arms to the side of the body.

Legs (Make 2)

R1: 6 sc in MR (6)
R2: inc in each st (12)
R3: (sc 1, inc 1) *6 (18)
R4-6: sc in each st (18)
Stuff the legs.
R7: (sc 1, dec 1) * 6 (12)
R8: dec * 6 (6)
R9: sc in each st (6)
FO leaving a long tail to sew. Attach the legs to the body.

Tail

R1: 6 sc in MR (6)
R2: inc in each st (12)
R3: sc in each st (12)
R4: dec * 6 (6)
FO leaving a long tail to sew. Attach the tail to the body.

Pumpkin Coffee Cozy

What You Need:
- 1 Category 4 yarn ball of medium weight yarn in Color A; here we will use Blue as Color A
- A small amount of lightweight yarn of category 4 in Color B; here we will use Orange for Color B
- A small amount of lightweight yarn of category 4 in Color C; here we will use Green as Color C
- Crochet hook of size 5.5 mm
- Crochet hook of size 3.75 mm
- Yarn needle used to thread ends
- A pair of single crochet scissors
- 1″ Button (Amy, 2013)

Cozy:

Use a crochet hook of size 5.5 mm and color A

Step 1: Make one chain 7

Step 2: Pull the loop out of the hook throughout the second ch

Step 3: Draw the loop for each of the next 4 stitches (you must be having 6 loops on the hook).

Step 4: Yarn over again and draw through all 6 loops on the hook (It's your first-star stitch) Make one chain to start closing the star (Which will be the "eye" of the star) (Amy, 2013)

Step 5: Insert your needle throughout the "eye" (ch 1 space) about your concluded star and grab the loop (2 loops on the hook)

Step 6: Introduce the hook well into the back of the last loop of the preceding star as well as draw the loop up (3 loops on the hook)

Step 7: Introduce the hook in the very same chain as the last loop of the recent star and pull the loop up (4 loops on the hook)

Step 8: For each of the next two chains, pull a loop (6 loops on the hook)

Step 9: Yarn over again and pull throughout all six loops. Make one chain to close down the star.

Reiterate steps 5-9 almost all of the way through and finish with 1 half double crochet over the last chain (same chain as that of the prior star's last loop) (6-star stitching)

Step 10: Make one chain. Ch. Switch on. Single Crochet at the top of this half double crochet.

Step 11: 1 single crochet in the "eye" of another star

Step 12: 2 single crochet in the eye for each star, all of the way through. 1 single crochet to the top of the crochet turning chain, turn this. (13 stitches)

Step 13: Chain 2, yarn over, hook in 2nd chain from hook, pull the loop up. For each of the next 3 stitches, pull a loop.

Step 14: Yarn over and pull the hook throughout all 6 loops. Chain 1 to close down the star.

Step 15: Proceed with both the star stitch (steps 5-9) almost all of the way to end with 1 half double crochet in the very same chain as the last loop of the earlier star.

Reiterate the steps form 11-15 ten times more, finishing with such a row of single crochet (I covered my cozy around my cup to decide the appropriate length. If your cozy is much too small to cover about your mug, incorporate couple more rows before you hit the perfect length).

Chain 1, switch 1 stitch crochet for each of the following 5 stitches, chain 3, skip 3 stitches, 1 single crochet in each of the final 5 stitches.

Single crochet out uniformly across the cozy whole. Fasten off with a yarn hook, and lace ends.

FOR PUMPKIN APPLIQUE:

Using a crochet hook of size F 3.75 mm and color B Magic circle. Chain 2, 12 double crochet within a magic circle, connect in the first double crochet with an sl st (not the ch 2.)

Chain 1, [1 half double crochet, 1 dc] into the first stitches, 2 double crochet into each of the next 3 stitches, 1 half double crochet into the next stitch, slip stitch into the next stitch, 1 half double crochet into the next stitch, 2 dc into each of the next 3 stitches, [1 dc, 1 half double crochet] into the next stitch, slip stitch into the last stitch. Fasten off, and leave for weaving a long tail.

Introduce Color C in the last stitch of the previous round.

Chain 3, 1 stitch into the hook's second chain and then the next stitch, slip stitch into the preceding round's finish stitch. Fasten off and finish weaving. (Amy, 2013)

Place your embroidery into the cozy middle. Check the cozy query. Tuck your cup comfortably to evaluate where your button should be located. Sew on and you're all finished!

And now your pattern is completed

Callie the Cat

This cartoon cat character is a lovable crochet toy that you can create for your kids. You can change the colors of the yarn to make her attractive. So go ahead and have fun creating this fantastic home buddy.

What You Need:
- DK/ worsted yarn in light grey (L), dark grey (D), black (B)
- 4 mm crochet hook
- A pair of 6 mm safety eyes
- Stuffing
- Embroidery needle to sew

Body

Use L
R1: 6 sc in MR (6)
R2: sc inc in each st (12)
R3: (sc in 1 st, sc inc 1) * 6 (18)
R4: (sc in 2 sts, sc inc 1) *6 (24)
R5: (sc in 3 sts, sc inc 1) *6 (30)
R6: (sc in 4 sts, sc inc 1) *6 (36)
R7: sc in 3 sts, CC D sc in 9 sts, CC L sc in 24 sts (36)
R8: sc in 3 sts, CC D sc in 10 sts, CC L sc in 23 sts (36)
R9–10: sc in each st (36)
R11: sc in 3 sts, CC D sc in 11 sts, CC L sc in 22 sts (36)
R12: sc in 3 sts, CC D sc in 12 sts, CC L sc in 21 sts (36)
R13–19: sc in each st (36)
Attach safety eyes.
R20: (sc in 4 sts, sc dec 1) * 6 (30)
R21: (sc in 3 sts, sc dec 1) * 6 (24)
R22: (sc in 2 sts, sc dec 1) * 6 (18)
R23: (sc in 1 st, sc dec 1) * 6 (12)
Stuff the head and continue working the body R24: (dec) * 6 (6)
Fasten off and weave in the ends.

Tail

Use D
R1: 6 sc in MR (6)
R2: (sc in 1 st, sc inc 1) * 3 (9)
CC L
R3–4: sc in each st (9)
CC D
R5–6: sc in each st (9)
CC L
R7–8: sc in each st (9)
CC D

R9: sc in each st (9)
Stuff the tail.
R10: (sc in 1 sts, sc dec 1) *3 (6)
Fasten off leaving a long tail to sew.
Attach the tail to the body.

Ears (Make 2)

Use L
R1: 3 sc in MR (3)
R2: sc inc in each st (6)
R3: sc in each st (6)
R4: (sc in 1 st, sc inc 1) * 3 (9)
Fasten off leaving a long tail to sew.
Attach the ears to the top of the body.

Feet (Make 4)

Use L
R1: 3 sc in MR (3)
R2: sc inc in each st (6)
Fasten off leaving a long tail to sew.
Attach the feet to the bottom of the body.
Using B embroider a mouth and whiskers.
Sew three straight stitches above the eyes with D.

Charlie the Dog

Now, who doesn't want their favorite pet as a toy? For those who cannot keep the real ones at home, this is the best option. So, make this cuddly dog and have fun playing with him for years. With his cute tongue sticking out, he will be a great companion all day long.

What You Need:
- DK/ worsted yarn in the color of your choice
- Red yarn
- 3.5 mm crochet hook
- A pair of 4 mm safety eyes

Stuffing

Embroidery needle to sew

Head

R1: 6 sc in MR (6)
R2: inc in each st (12)
R3: (sc 1, inc 1) * 6 (18)
R4: (sc 2, inc 1) * 6 (24)
R5–9: sc in each st (24)
R10: (sc 3, inc 1) * 6 (30)
R11: (sc 4, inc 1) * 6 (36)
R12: (sc 5, inc 1) * 5, sc 6 (41)
R13: (sc 6, inc 1) * 5, sc 6 (46)
R14: (sc 7, inc 1) * 5, sc 6 (51)
R15–17: sc in each st (51)
R18: (sc 7, dec 1) * 5, sc 6 (46)
R19: (sc 6, dec 1) * 5, sc 6 (41)
R20: (sc 5, dec 1) * 5, sc 6 (36)
R21: sc in each st (36)
R22: (sc 4, dec 1) *6 (30)
R23: (sc 3, dec 1) *6 (24)
R24: (sc 2, dec 1) *6 (18)
Attach safety eyes in place. Stuff the head.
R25: (sc 1, dec 1) * 6 (12)
R26: dec * 6 (6)
Fasten off and weave in the ends.
Using black yarn, sew a nose with straight stitches.

Ears (Make 2)

R1: 3 sc in MR (3)
R2: inc in each st (6)
R3: (sc 1, inc 1) * 3 (9)
R4: sc in each st (9)

R5: (sc 2, inc 1) * 3 (12)
R6: sc in each st (12)
R7: (sc 3, inc 1) * 3 (15)
R8: sc in each st (15)
R9: (sc 4, inc 1) * 3 (18)
R10–16: sc in each st (18)
Sew the open ends using sc. FO leaving a long tail to sew.
Sew the ears to the side of the head.

Body

R1: 8 sc in MR (8)
R2: inc in each st (16)
R3: (sc 1, inc 1) * 8 (24)
R4: (sc 2, inc 1) * 8 (32)
R5: (sc 3, inc 1) * 8 (40)
R6–17: sc in each st (40)
R18: (sc 3, dec 1) *8 (32)
R19–25: sc in each st (32)
R26: (sc 2, dec 1) * 8 (24)
R27: (sc 1, dec 1) * 8 (16)
Stuff the body.
R28: dec * 8 (8)
FO leaving a long tail to sew.
Attach the head to the body.

Legs (Make 4)

R1: 6 sc in MR (6)
R2: inc in each st (12)
R3: (sc 1, inc 1) * 6 (18)
R4: (sc 2, inc 1) * 6 (24)
R5–6: sc in each st (24)
R7: sc 12, (sc 2, dec 1) * 3 (21)
R8: sc 12, (sc 1, dec 1) * 3 (18)

R9: sc 12, (dec 1) * 3 (15)
R10–21: sc in each st (15)
Stuff the legs and FO leaving a long tail to sew.
Sew the legs closed and sew them in place on the body.

Tail

Ch 10, sc in 2nd ch from hook, sc, sc, hdc in 6 sts.
FO and sew the tail to the body.

Tongue

Use red yarn
R1: Ch 4, sc in 2nd ch from hook, sc, sc
R2: Ch1, turn, inc 1, sc, inc 1
R3: Ch1, turn, sc in each st
R4: Ch1, turn, dec 1, sc, dec 1
FO and sew to the muffle.

Greg the Lion

Your wild animal collection will not be complete without the king of the jungle. This lion pattern is simple and quick to make. The orange hair crocheted around the head gives it a royal look.

What You Need:

- DK/ worsted yarn in the color of your choice
- Orange and white yarn
- 4 mm crochet hook
- A pair of 6 mm safety eyes

Stuffing

Embroidery needle to sew

Head

R1: 6 sc in MR (6)
R2: sc inc in each st (12)
R3: (sc in 1 st, sc inc 1) * 6 (18)
R4:(sc in 2 sts, sc inc 1) *6 (24)
R5:(sc in 3 sts, sc inc 1) *6 (30)
R6:(sc in 4 sts, sc inc 1) *6 (36)
R7:(sc in 5 sts, sc inc 1) *6 (42)
R8: sc in each st (42)
R9:(sc in 6 sts, sc inc 1) *6 (48)
R10: sc in each st (48)
R11: (sc in 7 sts, sc inc 1) * 6 (54)
R12–17: sc in each st (54)
R18: (sc in 7 sts, sc dec 1) *6 (48)
R19: (sc in 6 sts, sc dec 1) *6 (42)
R20: (sc in 5 sts, sc dec 1) *6 (36)
R21: (sc in 4 sts, sc dec 1) * 6 (30)
R22: (sc in 3 sts, sc dec 1) * 6 (24)
Stuff the head.
FO leaving a long tail to sew.

Mouth

Use white yarn
R1: 6 sc in MR (6)
R2: sc inc in each st (12)
R3: (sc in 1 st, sc inc 1) * 6 (18)
R4: (sc in 2 sts, sc inc 1) * 6 (24)
R5–6: sc in each st (24)
FO leaving a long tail to sew.

With orange yarn, sew a nose and with black yarn sew the lips to the mouth. Stuff the mouth and attach the mouth to the head. Attach the safety eyes just above the mouth.

Body

R1: 6 sc in MR (6)
R2: sc inc in each st (12)
R3: (sc in 1 st, sc inc 1) * 6 (18)
R4: (sc in 2 sts, sc inc 1) * 6 (24)
R5: (sc in 3 sts, sc inc 1) * 6 (30)
R6–10: sc in each st (30)
R11: (sci n 3 sts, sc dec 1) *6 (24)
R12–14: sc in each st (24)
Stuff the body.
Using the yarn left from the head sew the body and head together at the open ends.

Legs (Make 2)

R1: ch 4, sc in 2nd ch from hook, sc, 3 sc in next st, (working backwards) sc, 2 sc in last st.
R2: sc inc 1, sc, (sc inc 1) * 3, sc, (sc inc 1) * 2
R3: sc inc1, sc, sc, (sc inc 1, sc) *3, sc, (sc inc 1, sc) *2
R4: sc in each st
R5: sc in 5 sts, (sc dec 1, sc in 2 sts) * 3, sc in 3 sts
R6: sc in 5 sts, (sc dec 1, sc in 1 st) * 3, sc in 3 sts
R7–8: sc in each st
FO leaving a long tail to sew.
Stuff the legs and attach them to the body.

Arms (Make 2)

R1: 6 sc in MR (6)
R2: sc inc in each st (12)
R3–9: sc in each st (12)

FO leaving a long tail to sew.
Stuff the arms and attach them to the body.

Tail

R1: Ch 15, sc in each ch.
FO leaving a long tail to sew.
Attach to the body.

Ears (Make 2)

R1: 6 sc in MR (6)
R2: sc inc in each st (12)
R3: (sc in 3 sts, sc inc 1) * 3 (15)
R4–5: sc in each st (15)
FO leaving a long tail to sew.
Attach to the head.
Using orange yarn, cut 4 5-inch strands.
Attach these to the tip of the tail using a knot.

Hair

Use orange yarn.
R1: Ch 60, turn
R2: sc in next st, (hdc in next st, {dc, tr, dc} in next st, hdc in next st, sl st in next st) * till the end.
FO leaving a long tail to sew.
Attach the hair around the head and secure it with straight stitches.

Benny the Bear

This bear pattern is an easy one to master. With this pattern, you can go ahead and personalize it to suit various styles. So, grab your hook and yarn, and create this stunning bear. Gift it to someone special or keep it for your very own collection.

What You Need:

- DK/ worsted yarn in the color of your choice
- 4 mm crochet hook

- A pair of 6 mm safety eyes

Stuffing

Embroidery needle to sew

Head

R1: 6 sc in MR (6)
R2: sc inc in each st (12)
R3: (sc in 1 st, sc inc 1) * 6 (18)
R4: (sc in 2 sts, sc inc 1) *6 (24)
R5: (sc in 3 sts, sc inc 1) *6 (30)
R6: (sc in 4 sts, sc inc 1) *6 (36)
R7: (sc in 5 sts, sc inc 1) *6 (42)
R8–13: sc in each st (42)
Attach eyes to the head at R9
R14: (sc in 5 sts, sc dec 1) * 6 (36)
R15: (sc in 4 sts, sc dec 1) * 6 (30)
R16: (sc in 3 sts, sc dec 1) * 6 (24)
R17: (sc in 2 sts, sc dec 1) * 6 (18)
Stuff the head.
R18: (sc in 1 st, sc dec 1) * 6 (12)
R19: dec in each st (6)
Fasten off and weave in the ends.

Mouth

R1: 6 sc in MR (6)
R2: sc inc in each st (12)
R3: (sc in 1 st, sc inc 1) * 6 (18)
R4–6: sc in each st (18)
R7: (sc in 1 st, sc dec 1) * 6 (12)
Stuff the mouth.
FO leaving a long tail to sew.

Sew the mouth to the front of the head. With black yarn sew a straight stitch on R2.

Body

R1: 6 sc in MR (6)
R2: sc inc in each st (12)
R3: (sc in 1 st, sc inc 1) * 6 (18)
R4: (sc in 2 sts, sc inc 1) *6 (24)
R5: (sc in 3 sts, sc inc 1) *6 (30)
R6: (sc in 4 sts, sc inc 1) *6 (36)
R7–12: sc in each st (36)
R13: (sc in 4 sts, sc dec 1) * 6 (30)
R14: (sc in 3 sts, sc dec 1) * 6 (24)
R15: (sc in 2 sts, sc dec 1) * 6 (18)
Stuff the body.
R16: (sc in 1 st, sc dec 1) * 6 (12)
R17: dec in each st (6)
Fasten off and weave in the ends.
Sew the head to the body.

Arms (Make 2)

R1: 6 sc in MR (6)
R2: sc inc in each st (12)
R3–4: sc in each st (12)
R5: (sc in 4 sts, sc dec 1) *2 (10)
R6–7: sc in each st (10)
R8: (sc in 3 sts, sc dec 1) *2 (8)
R9: sc in each st (8)
Stuff lightly.
FO leaving a long tail to sew.
Attach the arms to the sides of the body.

Legs (Make 2)

R1: 6 sc in MR (6)
R2: sc inc in each st (12)
R3–8: sc in each st (12)
R9: (sc in 1 st, sc dec 1) * 4 (8)
Stuff lightly.
FO leaving a long tail to sew.
Attach the legs to the sides of the body.

Ears (Make 2)

R1: 6 sc in MR (6)
R2: sc inc in each st (12)
R3: (sc in 1 st, sc inc 1) * 6 (18)
R4: (sc in 2 sts, sc inc 1) * 6 (24)
R5–7: sc in each st (24)
R8:(sc in 6 sts, sc dec 1) *3 (21)
R9: (sc in 5 sts, sc dec 1) *3 (18)
FO leaving a long tail to sew.
Attach the ears to the head.

Polly the Pig

A farm won't be complete without Polly the Pig. I chose the pink color but you can choose whatever color you like to add to your farm collection.

What You Need:

- DK/ worsted yarn in pink or color of your choice 50 g

- Black yarn
- 3.5 mm crochet hook
- A pair of 6 mm safety eyes

Stuffing

Embroidery needle to sew

Head & Body

R1: 6 sc in MR (6)
R2: (inc 1, sc 1) * 3 (9)
R3: (BLO) sc in each st (9)
R4: sc in each st (9)
R5: (inc 1, sc 2) *3 (12)
R6: sc in each st (12)
R7: (inc 1, sc 1) *6 (18)
R8:(inc1, sc2) *6 (24)
R9:(inc1, sc3) *6 (30)
R10: (inc 1, sc 9) * 3 (33)
You can now attach safety eyes between R7 and R8 with 6 sts in between.
R11–19: sc in each st (33)
R20: (dec 1, sc 9) * 3 (30)
R21: (dec 1, sc 3) * 6 (24)
Stuff the pig now and continue stuffing as you go.
R22: (dec 1, sc 2) * 6 (18)
R23: (dec 1, sc 1) * 6 (12)
R24: dec * 6 (6)
Stuff well. Fasten off and weave in the ends.

Tail

Chain 20.
Sl st in the second ch from hook and in the remaining 18 chains. FO leaving a long tail for sewing.

Attach the tail to the body at the center of R24.

Legs (Make 4)

R1: 6 sc in MR (6)
R2–3: sc in each st (6)
Sl st in next st.
FO leaving a long tail for sewing. Stuff the leg.
Once you create all 4 legs, sew on the two legs at R9 with 4 sts in between the two legs at R14 with 6 sts in between.

Ears (Make 2)

R1: 3 sc in MR, ch1, Turn (3)
R2: 2 sc in each of the 3 sts (6)
R3: 2 sc in MR (8)
FO leaving a long tail for sewing.
Sew the ears at R9 with 4 sts in between.

Finishing

Using black yarn, make small straight stitches for nostrils at R2.

Baby Monsters

What You Need:

- A Size E Crochet Hook (Or Your Choice Of Hook)
- A Little Amount Of Worsted Weight Yarn
- Polyester Fiberfill Stuffing
- Plastic Safety Eyes (About 6 Mm)

White Felt
Embroidery Floss
Scissors
Craft Glue
Embroidery Needle
Yarn Needle

Pattern for the Head and Body:

To start, make an adjustable ring with an E hook and worsted weight yarn at the top of the monster's head. Chain 1 and single crochet 6 stitches through the ring, pulling it closed in the loose yarn tail.

R1 (round 1): 2 sc (single crochet) into each st (stitch) (12)

R2: * (2 sc into next st, sc into next st) rep around (18)

R3: * (sc into next st, 2 sc into next st, sc into next st) rep around (24)

R4 to R12: sc into each st (24)

Fasten off and set aside.

Pattern for the Base:

Create an adjustable ring. Chain 1 and single crochet 6 stitches into the ring, pulling it closed.

R1: 2 sc into each st (12)

R2: * (2 sc into next st, sc into next st) rep to end of round (18)

R3: * sc into next st, 2 sc into next st, sc into next st) rep to end of round (24)

Fasten off.

Instructions for the Head and Body:

Put in the hook through the ring's front, hooking the working yarn. Take out a loop into the ring.

Enfold the working yarn or the yarn from the ball throughout the hook coming from the back and pull it into the loop on the hook. You should now have a chain stitch (ch).

Single crochet 6 stitches through the ring. Through the ring's forepart, insert the hook, pulling up a loop of your working yarn to the front. You should now have 2 loops on the hook.

From the back, enfold your working yarn all through the hook, pulling into the 2 loops. You should now have 1 single crochet (sc) stitch through the ring. Then, do another 5 sc stitches into the ring.

To close the ring, take out the short yarn tail so that the stitches tighten and form a round of stitches. You should now have the baby monster's base.

In order to enlarge the round/circle, you need to increase through crocheting twice for each stitch. Beneath both the loops of the following stitch, insert the hook. Then, take out a loop. You should now have 2 loops on the hook.

Wrapping the working yarn all over the hook, pull into the 2 loops. You now have 1 sc stitch. Do a single crochet through the same area, making an increase. In most patterns, it is written as "2 sc into next st." In this round, repeat the increase for each one stitch up to 12 stitches. You may determine the number of stitches through each "v" in the circle.

For the next round, do an increase alternating each stitch. You need to put 2 stitches in the 1st stitch, which means 1 stitch in the following stitch, then 2 stitches again in the following stitch, and so forth. You should have 18 stitches once you are done with this round.

For the final round, do an increase for every 3rd stitch. You need to single crochet twice in the 1st stitch and do a single crochet again once in the next 2 stitches. Then, single crochet twice in the following stitch and so forth. You should have 24 stitches in this round.

Once you are done increasing, you should come up with a flat circle that has 24 stitches all throughout. It could become cylindrical in shape once you single stitch around through every stitch for nine rows.

Crochet around the 24 stitches use a stitch marker and move it to the loop, which is upon the hook. Do this over again until you reach 9 rows. If you prefer a taller monster, you need to have more than 9 rows. If you prefer your monster to be shorter than the specified size in this pattern, you need to do less than 9 rows.

You should now finish the body of your monster with a slip stitch through the next stitch. You need to cut the yarn, leaving a few inches and insert the hook through the next stitch. Draw out a loop and take it out all throughout the loop on the hook.

Instructions for the Base:

In order to make the monster's base, you need to do the steps from the start to create a round or circle with 24 stitches. Prior to assembling the pieces together, you need to attach the monster's eye(s) by cutting the felt piece as you prefer. You could cut it into two small circles or just one big circle. Insert the eye in the spot that you desire by cutting a small slit to secure the eye. Put it wherever you want on the monster's body and push it through. Then, place the washer into the monster's body and secure it over the eye. Make sure to push hard so the washer snaps to the body all the way down.

Then, place a small quantity of stuffing inside the monster. Make sure the bottom part fits over the body's bottom part. Using a yarn needle and the long yarn tail, stitch all the parts of the monster together. Line the stitches up and sew between them. Once the hole closes, you may insert additional stuffing as you prefer.

Design the expression of your monster using embroidery floss and a needle for stitching the eyebrows, mouth, and eyelashes. You may add other features to the face of your monster. You may add a couple of teeth by cutting and gluing a piece of felt into the mouth.

Then, you may sew or glue the edges of the eyes. Tie a strand of yarn to come up with a bow, then stitch it on the head of the monster. It is best to use yarn with the same color as the monster's head. Then, you are done!

Buddy the Elephant

Required: about 20 g of Bernat Super Value (or similar weight yarn) in light grey, 5 g of dark grey. H or C hook (5 or 2.5 mm) depending on the preferred size of the toy, a pair of 10 mm safety eyes (I have the oval ones), a tapestry needle, polyester stuffing.

The body, head and trunk are made in one detail.

Rnd 1. with grey yarn:6 sc into MR (6)
Rnd 2. 6 inc (12)
Rnd 3. (Sc, inc) x 6 times (18)
Rnd 4. (2 sc, inc) x 6 times (24)
Rnd 5. (3 sc, inc) x 6 times (30)
Rnd 6. (4 sc, inc) x 6 times (36)
Rnd 7. (5 sc, inc) x 6 times (42)

Rnd 8-17. 42 sc.
Keep working with one color if you want your elephant to be unicolored.

Or give your guy some colorful stripes while working rounds 8-17. I chose some dark grey stripes for my boy; you can go even with rainbow colors.

Rnd 18. (5 sc, dec) x 6 times (36)
Rnd 19. 36 sc
Rnd 20. (4 sc, dec) x 6 times (24). Insert safety eyes at rounds 19-20.
Rnd 21. 24 sc
Rnd 22. (3 sc, dec) x 6 times (18), Begin with stuffing.
Rnd 23-24.18 sc
Rnd 25. (4 sc, dec) x 3 times (15)
Rnd 26-27. 15 sc
Rnd 28. (3 sc, dec) x 3 times (12)
Rnd 29-30. 12 sc. Continue stuffing as you go.
Rnd 31. (2 sc, dec) x 3 times (9)
Rnd 32-33. 9 sc
Rnd 34. (Sc, dec) x 3 times (6)

Rnd 35-37. 6 sc
Rnd 38. (Sc, dec) x 2 times (4)
Make 2-3 rounds of 4 sc with no stuffing.

Ears (make 2)

Please note we will also use DC along with regular SC here

Rnd 1. with dark grey yarn: 6 sc into MR (6)
Rnd 2. 6 inc (12). Change to light grey color. The first picture shows how to properly add another color.
Rnd 3. (sc, inc) x 6 times (18)
Rnd 4. (2 sc, inc) x 6 times (24)
Rnd 5. (3 sc, inc) x 6 times (30). Change back to dark grey if you want it decolored or skip it if you prefer one color.
Rnd 6. 6 sc, (4 dc, inc) x 5 times, (36)
Fasten off and cut the yarn with a long end to sew it

Attach the ears as shown in the picture. The side with 5 sc will go to the body.

Back legs (make 2)

Rnd 1. 6 sc into MR (6)
Rnd 2. 6 inc (12).
Rnd 3. 12 sc in BLO
Rnd 4-10. 12 sc,
Fasten off and cut the yarn with a long end to sew it. Front legs are just 1 round shorter than the pair of back legs.
Stuff all legs firmly.

Tail

Combine 2 strands of dark and light grey yarn (or just 2 strands of the main color) and make ch 10.
The Elephant is done!

Holly the Hippo

Holly the Hippo is a simple yet fun pattern that you can create easily. With a large head, she demands attention from all around her. Try out various colors of yarn to make her colorful and fun to play with.

What You Need:

- DK/ worsted yarn in the color of your choice
- Pink yarn
- 4 mm crochet hook
- A pair of 6mm safety eyes

Stuffing

Embroidery needle to sew

Head

Ch 4
R1: 2 sc in 2nd ch from hook, sc, 3 sc in last ch.
Working along the back of the chain, sc, sc (8)
R2: inc 1 in first sc, inc 1, sc, inc 1, inc 1, inc 1, sc, inc 1 (14)
R3: inc 1 in first sc, inc 1, sc in next 4 sc, inc 1, inc 1, inc 1, sc in next 4 sc, inc 1. (20)
R4–7: sc in each sc (20) R8:(dec 1, dec 1, sc in next 6 sc) *2 (16)
R9: (dec 1, sc in next 6 sc) * 2 (14)
R10-11: sc in each st (14)

Stuff the body

R12: (dec 1, sc 2) * around and end with dec 1 in last 2 sc (10)
R13: dec in each st (5)
Fasten off and weave in the ends.

Body

R1: 5 sc in MR (5)
R2: inc in each st (10)
R3: (sc 1, inc 1) *5 (15)
R4: (sc 2, inc 1) *5 (20)
R5: (sc 3, inc 1) *5 (25)
R6–8: sc in each st (25)
R9: (sc 3, dec 1) * 5 (20)
R10–12: sc in each st (20)
R13: (dec 1, sc 2) * 5 (15)
FO leaving a long tail to sew. Sew head to the body.

Ears (Make 2)

R1: 6 sc in MR (6)
R2: inc in each st (12)
FO leaving a long tail to sew.

Sew ears to head.
Using pink yarn, embroider straight and stitch for nostrils.

Legs (Make 4)

R1: 6 sc in MR (6)
R2–4: sc in each st (6)
FO leaving a long tail to sew. Sew the legs to the body.

Tail

Ch 4, sl st in 2nd ch from hook, sc, sc.
Fasten off and weave in the ends.
Sew tail to body.

Dress Up

What You Need:

- Crochet Hook (4.5 Mm)
- Red Heart Comfort Yarn (Any Color) Or Yarn With The Same Weight
- Scissors
- Yarn Needle (Blunt End; For Sewing)

Abbreviations in the Pattern:

sc – single crochet
st – stitch
f/o – finish off
Note: In this pattern, every row follows a sequence. The number in the parentheses is referred to as the number of stitches that you need to achieve at the end of a specific row.

Pattern for the Dress:

R1: ch 19
R2: begin with the 2nd ch from hook; work 1 single crochet in each ch (18) ch 1 turn
R3: skip ch; work 1 single crochet in next 3 stitches; ch 4; single crochet in the 4th stitch from the beginning of ch; 1 single crochet in next 4 stitches; ch 4; sc into 4th stitch from eh beginning of ch; 1 single crochet in next 3 stitches (18); ch 1 turn
R4: skip ch; 1 single crochet in each stitch (18); ch 1 turn
R5: skip ch; 1 single crochet in next 5 stitches; 2 sc in next stitch (21); ch 1 turn
R6: skip ch; 1 single crochet in next 6 stitches; 2 sc in next stitch (24); ch 1 turn
R7: skip ch; 1 single crochet in the first stitch; ch 3; single crochet in next stitch; repeat ch 3; single crochet in next stitch until the last stitch of the row is reached; put 1 single crochet in the last stitch.

Finish off. Leave a long tail and sew the back edges together. Leave it open near the top of the dress to allow easy placement on and off the doll. Add a button of your choice. Loop to close the top.

Pattern for the Bow:

R1: ch 2
R2: work 4 sc in the 2nd chain from the hook; slip stitch in 1st stitch; pull starting yarn tail to close hole
R3: ch 2

R4: work 4 sc in the 2nd chain from the hook.

Finish off. Leave a long tail and wrap it around the middle. Knot off using the starting yarn tail.

Instructions for the Bow Strap:

Push the hook into any yarn in the bow's back, pulling the finishing yarn tail through. Ch 10 and finish off. Sew the end to the start of the chain. Weave yarn tails.

Pattern for the Purse:

R1: ch 6
R2: start in 2nd ch; work 1 single crochet in each chain (5); ch 1 turn
R3: skip ch; work 1 single crochet in each stitch (5); ch 1 turn
R4: skip ch; work 1 single crochet in each stitch (5); ch 1 turn
R5: skip ch; work 1 single crochet in each of the BLO (5); ch 1 turn
R6: skip ch; work 1 single crochet in each stitch; ch 1 turn
R7: skip ch; work 1 single crochet in each stitch
R8: ch 11; work slip stitch into the opposite corner

Finish off. Leave a long tail, fold the purse, and sew edges to close off. Weave yarn tails.

Pattern for the Overalls:

R1: ch 23
R2: start in 2nd ch; work 1 single crochet in each chain (22); ch 1 turn
R3: skip ch; work 1 single crochet in each stitch (22); ch 1 turn
R4: skip ch; work 1 single crochet in each stitch (22); ch 1 turn
Hold ends and connect with a single crochet. Use a stitch marker in the connecting stitch and move it to the last stitch you make for every completed row.
R5: work 1 single crochet in each stitch for 1 row (22)

R6: work 1 single crochet in the next 3 stitches; work 2 sc in the next stitch; repeat sequence to the last 2 stitches of the row; put 1 single crochet in the last 2 stitches (27)
R7: work 1 single crochet in each stitch for 1 row

Note: Do not break free as this would follow making the leg holes.

Instructions for the First Leg:

Use a stitch marker in the last stitch you made. The marked stitched will be the basis upon reaching the end of row 8. Skip the next 12 stitches and put 1 single crochet through the 13 stitches. You should now have 14 stitches, including the marked stitch for one leg hold. The 13 stitches are for the other; however, they would look even when everything is done.
Work to the left. The back of the overalls should be facing you. Work 1 single crochet in each of the next 12 outer loops. Work 1 single crochet in the inner loop containing the marker. Move the marker. Work 1 single crochet in the next 13 outer loops. Do a slip stitch in both loops of the marked stitch. Finish off and weave yarn tail.

Instructions for the Second Leg:

Turn the overalls so that it faces you. Insert yarn through the utmost corner. Ch 1 and use a stitch marker onto it. Skip ch when you reach the last row. Work to the right. Work 1 single crochet in each of the outer loops for 2 rows. Do a slip stitch on both loops of the last stitch of row 11. Finish off and weave yarn tails.

Pattern for the Bib:

R1: ch 7
R2: start in 2nd ch; work 1 single crochet in each chain (6); ch 1 turn
R3: skip ch; work 1 single crochet in each stitch (6); ch 1 turn
R4: skip ch; work 1 single crochet in each stitch (6); ch 1 turn
R5: skip ch; work 1 single crochet in each stitch (6)
Finish off. Leave a long tail.

Pattern for the Straps:

R1: ch 12
R2: start in 2nd ch; work 1 single crochet in each chain (11) Finish off. Leave a long tail and weave starting yarn tail through the strap. Sew the straps to the overalls using the finishing yarn.

Instructions for the Assembly of the Overalls:

In the back of the overalls, sew 2 open ends together. Make sure to sew only the corners on the top, leaving a hole for the tail of the mouse. Weave yarn tail.

The end of each strap should be sewn to the bib. There should be enough to overlap the ends. Make sure that the overlap is on the bib's inner part to hid the overlap once the doll wears the bib. Weave the yarn tail by the strap to the other end, stretching out the strap. Knot the yarn tail at the end. Using this yarn tail, sew the other end, then weave the other yarn tail to hide it.

Sew the bib to the center and the front of the overalls and weave yarn tails. To the back, sew the straps to the overalls. There should be a slight overlap. If you are unsure with the amount or size of the overlap, you can simply wear the overalls on the doll to measure. Weave yarn tails.

Serena the Starfish

This cute little starfish is waiting to be played with. You can create him in any color you use. This starfish is made by joining two pieces together and stuffing the whole. Sew a smile on his face and let him brighten up your day.

What You Need:

- DK/ worsted yarn in the color of your choice 50g
- Black yarn
- 3 mm and 3.5 mm crochet hook

Stuffing

Embroidery needle to sew

Body (Make 2)

Using a 3.5 mm hook
R1: 5 sc in MR (5)
R2: 2 sc in each st (10)
R3: (sc 1, inc 1) *5 (15)
R4: (sc 2, inc 1) *5 (20)
R5: (sc 3, inc 1) *5 (25)
Now change to a 3 mm hook
R6: (Ch 14, sl st into the 2nd ch from hook, sl st, 2 sc, 4 hdc, 4 dc, 1 tr, sl st in the next 4 sts of the body) * 5
R7: (1 tr in the first st on the arm, 4 dc, 4 hdc, 2 sc, 2 sl st, continue to sl st in the sts of R6 till you reach the next arm) * 5 [Figures below]
Do not FO.

Assembly

Keeping the two pieces together, sl st around the edges while stuffing as you go.
Using black yarn, embroider eyes and mouth.

Casper the Octopus

Casper is a cute little octopus that you can complete in no time. A stuffed body and simple tentacles—this pattern couldn't have been easier. Choose any color you like and make her as bright as possible.

What You Need:

- DK/ worsted yarn in the color of your choice 50g
- Scraps of white yarn
- Black yarn
- 3.5 mm crochet hook

- A pair of 6 mm safety eyes

Stuffing

Embroidery needle to sew

Body

Use yarn color of your choice
R1: 6 sc in MR (6)
R2: inc in each st (12)
R3: (sc1, inc 1) *6 (18)
R4: (sc 2, inc 1) *6 (24)
R5: (sc 3, inc 1) *6 (30)
R6: (sc 4, inc 1) *6 (36)
R7: (sc 5, inc 1) *6 (42)
R8–13: sc in each st (42)
R14: (sc 5, dec 1) *6 (36)
R15: (sc 4, dec 1) *6 (30)
You can now attach the eyes between R12 and R13 with 8 sts in between. Using black yarn, sew a mouth on R14.
R16: (sc 3, dec 1) *6 (24)
R17: (sc 2, dec 1) *6 (18)

Stuff the body

R18: (sc 1, dec 1) *6 (12)
R19: dec in each st (6)
FO leaving a long tail to sew.

Tentacles (Make 8)

This is made with two pieces sewn together: one in the main color and one in white.
With white yarn:
R1: Ch 20, turn
R2: sc in 2nd ch from hook, sc in next, hdc in 17 sts FO.

Repeat the same with yarn in the main color but do not FO. Keep the pieces together and then sc in 18, 3 sc, sc in 18. Leave a long tail to sew.

Assembly

Sew the tentacles on the head around R5.

Jenny the Jellyfish

A variation of the octopus pattern, this jellyfish will be another cool addition to your collection. Make many of them in various colors. They are absolutely cute and can be used as keychains, as well.

What You Need:

- DK/ worsted yarn in the color of your choice 50g
- Black yarn
- 3.5 mm crochet hook
- A pair of 9 mm safety eyes

Stuffing

Embroidery needle to sew

Body

Use yarn color of your choice
R1: 6 sc in MR (6)
R2: inc in each st (12)
R3: (sc 1, inc 1) *6 (18)
R4: (sc 2, inc 1) *6 (24)
R5: (sc 3, inc 1) *6 (30)
R6: (sc 4, inc 1) *6 (36)
R7: (sc 5, inc 1) *6 (42)
R8–13: sc in each st (42)
R14: BLO (sc 5, dec 1) * 6 (36)
R15: (sc 4, dec 1) * 6 (30)
You can now attach the eyes between R12 and R13 with 8 sts in between.
Using black yarn sew a mouth on R14.
R16: (sc 3, dec 1) *6 (24)
R17: (sc 2, dec 1) *6 (18)

Stuff the body

R18: (sc 1, dec 1) *6 (12)
R19: dec in each st (6)
FO leaving a long tail to sew.

Skirt

Using the front loops of R14, attach yarn to any of the sts.
Ch 3, 2 dc in the same st, skip 1 sc, sc in the next, (skip 1 sc, 5 dc in next sc, skip 1 sc, sc in next) * repeat around, 2 dc in first st, sl st to top of ch 3.
FO.

Tentacles (Make 3)

Ch 31, 2 sc in 2nd ch from hook, 3 sc in every remaining st. FO leaving a long tail to sew.

Assembly

Sew the tentacles to the center of the body base.

Wally the Whale

Wally is a tiny whale with a large heart! This quick-to-make pattern will have you creating several of them in no time. Attach safety eyes or glue on googly eyes for that impressive look. Choose colors of your choice to make Wally the Whale.

What You Need:
- DK/worsted yarn in blue and white
- 3.5 mm crochet hook
- A pair of 9 mm safety eyes

Stuffing

Embroidery needle to sew

Body

Use blue yarn
R1: 6 sc in MR (6)
R2: inc in each st (12)
R3: (sc 1, inc 1) *6 (18)
R4: (sc 2, inc 1) *6 (24)
R5: (sc 3, inc 1) *6 (30)
R6: (sc 4, inc 1) *6 (36)
R7: (sc 5, inc 1) *6 (42)
R8: (sc 6, inc 1) *6 (48)
R9: (sc 7, inc 1) *6 (54)
R10–20: sc in each (54)
R21: (sc 7, dec 1) * 6 (48)
Change to white yarn.
R22: sc in each st (48)
R23: (sc 4, dec 1) *8 (40)
R24: (sc 2, dec 1) *8 (30)
R25: (sc 1, dec 1) *8 (20)

Stuff the body

R26: dec in all st (10)
R27: dec in all st (5)
FO.

Fins (Make 2)

Use blue yarn.
R1: 6 sc in MR (6)
R2: inc in each st (12)
R3–6: sc in each st (12)
Fold and sc across to close the gap.

FO leaving a long tail to sew.
Sew the fins to the side of the body at R27.

Tail

Use blue yarn.
Make 2
R1: 6 sc in MR (6)
R2: inc in each st (12)
R3–6: sc in each st (12)
Fold and sc across to close the gap.
FO
Join the two tail pieces at the R1 edge to form a V shape tail. Sew this tail to the body at R27.

Phoebe the Turtle

Another cute pattern those kids will love! Phoebe is simple enough to create and can be either made with a single color or multiple colors. Phoebe is small in size but packs a punch. You can make him larger in size by just using larger size hooks.

What You Need:
- DK/ worsted yarn in colors of your choice (B for color1, W for color2)
- 3.5 mm crochet hook
- A pair of 9 mm safety eyes

Stuffing

Embroidery needle to sew

Body

Use B.
R1: 6 sc in MR (6)
Change to W.
R2: inc in each st (12)
Change to B.
R3: (sc 1, inc 1) * 6 (18)
Change to W.
R4: sc in each st (18)
Change to B.
R5: (sc 2, inc 1) * 6 (24)
Change to W.
R6: sc in each st (24)
Change to B.
R7: (sc 3, inc 1) * 6 (30)
Change to W.
R8: sc in each st (30)
Change to B.
R9: sc in each st (30)
Change to W.
R10: sc in each st (30)
R11: BLO (sc 3, dec 1) * 6 (24)
R12: (sc 2, dec 1) * 6 (18)
Stuff the body.
R13: (sc 1, dec 1) * 6 (12)
R14: dec in each st (6)
Fasten off and weave in the ends.

Head

Use white yarn.

R1: 6 sc in MR (6)
R2: inc in each st (12)
R3: (sc 1, inc 1) *6 (18)
R4: (sc 2, inc 1) *6 (24)
R5–7: sc in each st (24)
R8: (sc 2, dec 1) * 6 (18)
Attach the eyes at R6.
R9: sc in each st (18)
R10: (sc 1, dec 1) * 6 (12)
FO leaving a long tail to sew.
Stuff the head and sew it to the body.

Legs (Make 4)

Use white yarn.
R1: 6 sc in MR (6)
R2–3: sc in each st (6)
FO leaving a long tail to sew. Sew the legs to the body at R11.

Tail

Use white yarn.
Ch4, sl st in 2nd ch from hook, sl st, sc.
FO leaving a long tail to sew.
Sew the tail to the body at R11.

Cinderella

Materials

- A Size E Crochet Hook (Or Your Choice of Hook)
- Yarn
- Polyester Fiberfill Stuffing
- Plastic Safety Eyes (About 6 Mm)
- White Felt
- Embroidery Floss
- Scissors
- Craft Glue
- Embroidery Needle
- Yarn Needle

This pattern is a bit more difficult than the previous ones, but if you pay attention to details, you will succeed in making your very own Cinderella. There is a lot of detailing, but overall, it is a pretty straightforward pattern. You can change the details to make whatever other Disney princess you want. With different colors and a bit of difference in stitches, you can make it, I'm sure.

So, we will start off with making the head. You will use skin color for the head part. To begin, you will make a magic ring and work six sc into the ring. Then, you will increase each of the stitches. As you probably guess, you will now gradually increase the size by one Next, we will be making the legs and the body. You will make two of the following. Using white yarn, you will make a magic ring and work six sc into the ring. Work sc around for the next five rounds. You will stuff the legs gently. Once you finish the second leg, you will leave the yarn to keep working on the body. So, in the seventh round, you will chain three and join the first leg.

Crochet six sc around the first leg, three sc in the chain three from before, six sc around the second leg and three sc on the other side of the chain three. In the next three rounds, sc all stitches. Change the color of your yarn to blue and sc all around for the next two rounds. In the 13th round, you will sc in back loops all around and in the 14th, you will sc all stitches. Then, you will change the color of the skin and sc all around. In the 16th round, you will alternate one sc, one decrease. Then change the color to black and sc all the 12 stitches. Then, you will fasten off the yarn and stuff the body.

Next, we're making arms. Using white yarn, you will make the magic ring and sc into the ring. For the next three rounds, you will sc all around. Change color to skin and sc all around for the next three rounds. Fasten off the yarn and in doing so, leave a long tail. You don't need to stuff the arms. For the sleeves, chain nine and in the second chain from the hook slip stitch twice, sc four times and work another two slip stitches.

Fasten off the yarn. You will repeat this for the other hand and sleeve.

Next, we're going to make the hair. Using yellow yarn, you will make the magic ring and work six sc into the ring. Next, increase all around. In the third round, you will alternate one sc, one increase. In the following three rounds, you will increase by crocheting two sc, increase, three sc, increase and four sc, increase respectively.

For the next three rounds, you will sc all around. In the next round, you will skip one, crochet five double crochet (dc), skip one and you will repeat it five times. Then, you will work one sc, chain one and turn. For the next seven rows, you will work 16 sc, chain one and turn every time. Then you will fasten off the yarn with a long tail. For the bun, you will make a magic ring and work six sc into the ring. Next, increase all around. In the next round, you will alternate one sc, one increase and in the round after you will work two sc and one increase all around. For the next five rounds, you will work sc all around. Fasten off the yarn with a long tail. For the headband, you will chain 25 using blue yarn. Next, you will do one slip stitch, three dc, two sc, one half-double crochet (hdc), 10 dc, one hdc, two sc and four slip stitches at the end. Fasten off the yarn with a long tail. Lastly, we will make the dress skirt. Using the blue yarn you will go back to round 13 of the body. In the first round of the skirt, you will chain three in the front loops, and then repeat until the end of the round the following: four dc, two dc and slip stitch at the end of the round.

For the next four rounds, you will chain three and work dc all around, joining with a slip stitch. Fasten off and weave in the ends. For the dress band, we will use white color. Chain 26 and work one slip stitch in the second chain, then two sc, and then one hdc and one dc in the same stitch.

Then you will work one dc; two half treble crochet (htr) in the same stitch; three treble crochet (tc) in the same stitch; two htr in the same stitch; one dc; one dc, one hdc in the same stitch; one sc; three slip stitches; two sc; one hdc, one dc in the same stitch; one dc; two htr in the same stitch; three tc in the same stitch; two htr in the same stitch; one dc; one dc, one hdc in the same stitch; one sc; one slip stitch. Fasten off the yarn.

All you have to do now is to assemble the parts. Attach the head to the body. Sew on the hands and sleeves, as well as the hair, bun, headband and dress band. It is all just simple sewing on. When you're finished with sewing, weave in the ends and that's it! Congratulations!

Tommy the Crab

Tommy is a chubby little crab all ready to play with you. Make her in any color you like but red is her favorite. The pattern is a very simple one with a little bit of work on the claws. Try out this amigurumi pattern today.

What You Need:

- DK/ worsted yarn in the color of your choice
- 3.5 mm crochet hook
- A pair of 6 mm safety eyes

Stuffing

Embroidery needle to sew

Body

R1: 6 sc in MR (6)
R2: inc in each st (12)
R3: (sc 1, inc 1) *6 (18)
R4: (sc 2, inc 1) *6 (24)
R5: (sc 3, inc 1) *6 (30)
R6: (sc 4, inc 1) *6 (36)
R7–8: sc in each st (36)
R9: (sc 4, dec 1) * 6 (30)
R10: (sc 3, dec 1) * 6 (24)
R11: (sc 2, dec 1) * 6 (18)
R12: (sc 1, dec 1) * 6 (12)
R13: dec * 6 (6)
Stuff the body. Fasten off and weave in the ends.

Legs (Make 4-6)

R1: 5 sc in MR (5)
R2–7: sc in each st (5)
FO leaving a long tail to sew. Sew the legs to the body.

Claws (Make 2)

R1: 4 sc in MR (4)
R2: (sc 1, inc 1) * 2 (6)
R3: (sc 2, inc 1) * 2 (8)
R4: sc in each st (8)
R5: (sc 3, inc 1) * 2 (10)
R6: Ch 3, sc in the 2nd ch from hook, sc in next st, now working on the sts of R5—sc in each st ending with an sc under the triangular piece just made.
R7: sc 5, dec 1, sc 4 (10)

R8: sc 5, dec 1, sc 3 (9)
R9: dec 1, sc 3, dec 1, sc 2 (7)
R10: dec 1, sc 2, dec 1, sc 1 (5)
R11–14: sc in each st (5)
FO leaving a long tail to sew.
Sew the claws on the body. Sew eyes on the body at R7.

Max the Clown Fish

Doesn't Max look adorable?? Grab your supplies and let's get started on this funny little clownfish. With bright orange and white yarn and bulging eyes, Max is all set to impress you. This is an easy pattern to follow that includes color changing.

What You Need:

- DK/ worsted yarn in orange, white and black
- 3.5 mm crochet hook
- A pair of 6 mm safety eyes

Stuffing

Embroidery needle to sew

Body

Use orange yarn.
R1: 6 sc in MR (6)
R2: inc in each st (12)
R3: (sc 1, inc 1) * 6 (18)
R4: (sc 2, inc 1) * 6 (24)
R5: (sc 3, inc 1) * 6 (30)
R6–7: sc in each st (30)
R8: (sc 4, inc 1) * 6 (36)
Change to black yarn.
Place eyes at R4 with 5 sts in between.
R9: sc in each st (36)
Change to white yarn.
R10–11: sc in each st (36)
Change to black yarn.
R12: sc in each st (36)
Change to orange yarn.
R13: sc in each st (36)
R14: (sc 4, dec 1) *6 (30)
R15–16: sc in each st (30)
Change to black.
R17: sc in each st (30)
Change to white.
R18: (sc 3, dec 1) *6 (24)
Change to black.
R19: sc in each st (24)
Change to orange yarn.
R20: sc in each st (24)
R21: (sc 2, dec 1) * 6 (18)
R22: sc in each st (18)
Change to black yarn.
R23: sc in each st (18)
Change to white.

R24: sc in each st (18)
R25: (sc 1, dec 1) *6 (12)
R26: dec * 6 (6)
Fasten off and weave in the ends.

Fins (Make 3)

Use orange yarn.
R1: Ch 7, sc in 2nd ch from hook, sc in next 5 st
R2: Turn, ch1, sc in each st
R3: Turn, ch1, sc in first 2 st, dec 1, sc in last 2 sts
R4–5: Turn, ch1, sc in each st
R6: Turn, ch1, dec 1, sc 1, dec 1
FO leaving a long tail to sew.
Attach one fin to each side of the body at R12. Attach the third fin to the back of the body.

Dorsal Fin

Use orange yarn.
R1: Ch10, sc in 2nd ch from hook, sc in next 8 st
R2: Turn, ch1, sc, hdc, dc, hdc, sc, sc, hdc, hdc, sc
R3: Turn, ch1, sc, hdc, hdc, sc, sc, hdc, dc, hdc, sc
R4: sc, sc
FO leaving a long tail to sew.
Attach the fin to the top of the body.

Eyes (Make 2)

Use white yarn.
R1: 6sc in MR (6)
R2: inc in each st (12)
R3: (sc 1, inc 1) * 6 (18)
FO leaving a long tail to sew.
With the wrong side facing out, attach the safety eyes, one inside of each crocheted eye, and sew them in place on the body.

Sew a mouth using black yarn below the eyes.

Pinky the Mouse

What You Need:

- 10-15 g of any bright acrylic yarn, (I used BERNAT Premium)
- H hook (5 mm)
- A pair of 10 mm safety eyes, tapestry needle, polyester stuffing.

Please remember to leave long ends at the beginning and the end: we will use them later for Pinky's tail.

Rnd 1. with main color: 8 sc into MR (8)
Rnd 2. 8 inc (16)
Rnd 3. (sc, inc) x 8 times (24)
Rnd 4. (2 sc, inc) x 8 times (32)
Rnd 5. (3 sc, inc) x 8 times (40)
Rnd 6-10. 40 sc
Rnd 11. (3 sc, dec) x 8 times (32)
Rnd 12. 32 sc
Rnd 13. (2 sc, dec) x 8 times (24)
Rnd 14-15. 24 sc

Insert a pair of safety eyes in round 16 and begin stuffing.
Rnd 16. (4 sc, dec) x 4 imes (20)
Rnd 17. 20 sc
Rnd 18. (3 sc, dec) x 4 times (16)

Rnd 19. (2 sc, dec) x 4 times (12). Add some more stuffing if needed.
Rnd 20. 6 dec (6). Fasten off leaving a long end.
Make a few stitches with black yarn for the nose as shown in the picture

Ears (make 2)

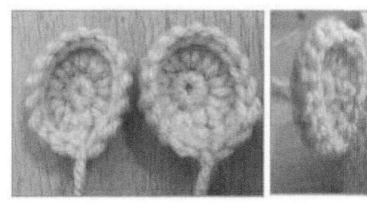

Rnd 1. Make 8 sc in MR, sl st to join and ch2 (8)
Rnd 2. 8 hdc inc, sl st to join and ch1 (16)
Rnd 3. 16 sc, sl st to join.

Tighten the MR and pull both ends (start of MR and end of work) through the whole body onto the 1st MR to form the tail later.
Sew both ears on the sides of the face as shown in the picture.

Tail

We ended up having 6 long ends coming out of the initial MR: 1 from the start and another one from the final round, where you fastened the yarn off, 2 from each ear. Take 2 ends as 1 strand and make a nice and long braided tail.

Make a few stitches with black yarn for his whiskers and our Mr. Mouse is done!

Teddy the Sloth

Required: 20 g of Bernat Super Value (or similar weight yarn) in coffee or any light brown, 5-8 g of white or off-white for the face, 5 g of dark brown for eyes pieces, H and C hook (5 and 2.5 mm) a pair of 10 mm safety eyes, tapestry needle, polyester stuffing.
We will use a smaller hook C for eye pieces.

Head

Rnd 1. with off-white yarn: 6 sc into MR (6)
Rnd 2. 6 inc (12)
Rnd 3. (sc, inc) x 6 times (18)
Rnd 4. 18 sc
Rnd 5. (2 sc, inc) x 6 times (24)
Rnd 6. 24 sc
Rnd 7. (3 sc, inc) x 6 times (30)
Rnd 8. (4 sc, inc) x 6 times (36)
Rnd 9. (5 sc, inc) x 6 times (42). Change to light brown (mail color).
Rnd 10. (6 sc, inc) x 6 times (48)

Rnd 11-14. 48 sc
Rnd 15. (6 sc, dec) x 6 times (42)
Rnd 16. (5 sc, dec) x 6 times (36)
Rnd 17. (4 sc, dec) x 6 times (30)
Rnd 18. (3 sc, dec) x 6 times (24). Begin stuffing and continue as you go.
You should make a pair of dark brown eye pieces before closing the head completely.
Rnd 19. (2 sc, dec) x 6 times (18)
Rnd 20. (1 sc, dec) x 6 times (12)
Rnd 21. 6 dec (6)
Make a few stitches to embroider the nose between the eyes as in the picture.

Eye piece (make 2 with dark brown color)

With a smaller hook (I used 2.5 mm) make chain 8
Starting from the 2nd chain from the hook make 2 sc dc, 4 dctog in the last chain. Turn to the other side of the chain and make 4 dc, 1 sc, 2 sc tog in the last loop the 1st pic below shows 4 dctog in the last chain and turn to the other side of the chain. You can see the completed 1st round on the 2nd pic.

Rnd 2. 3 sc, 4 dc, 4 dc inc in the next 4 stitches, 4 dc, 1 sc, 2 sc inc, ss in the last.

Insert your safety eyes right into the turning point of the 1st round (there's a bigger hole there) and onto the head of the sloth. Put a safety cap from inside of the head to secure it. Sew the eye pieces to the face with the narrower part pointing slightly down.

Body

Rnd 1. with light brown yarn: 6 sc into MR (6)
Rnd 2. 6 inc (12)
Rnd 3. (sc, inc) x 6 times (18)
Rnd 4. (2 sc, inc) x 6 times (24)
Rnd 5. (3 sc, inc) x 6 times (30)
Rnd 6. (4 sc, inc) x 6 times (36)
Rnd 7. (5 sc, inc) x 6 times (42)
Rnd 8-13. 42 sc
Rnd 14. (5 sc, dec) x 6 times (36)
Rnd 15. 36 sc
Rnd 16. (4 sc, dec) x 6 times (30)
Rnd 17. 30 sc. Begin stuffing.
Rnd 18. (2 sc, inc) x 6 times (24)
Rnd 19-20. 24 sc. Begin stuffing and keep doing as you go.
Rnd 21. (sc, inc) x 6 times (18)
Rnd 22-23. 18 sc
Fasten off and cut the yarn.

Arm/legs (make 4)

Rnd 1. with main color: 6 sc into MR (6)
Rnd 2. 6 inc (12)
Rnd 3. (sc, inc) x 6 times (18)

Rnd 4-6. 18 sc
Rnd 7. (1 sc, dec) x 6 times (12)
Rnd 8-20. 12 sc
Cut the yarn and fasten off leaving enough yarn for sewing. See the picture below for the correct placement of arms.
Stuff the limbs loosely and sew them to the body as shown.

Your lazy sloth is done!

Jimmy the Owl

You can make this cute little owl with both eyes closed or open as you prefer. I've made the eyes differently to show both options for you.

Required: You will need about 10g of blue acrylic yarn for the body, a couple of grams of yellow yarn for the wings and the beak, a few grams of off-white yarn for the eyes and a few cm of black yarn if you decide to embroider the sleepy eyes (I used BERNAT Premium), 2,50 mm crochet hook (US size 2/C), a pair of safety eyes if you go with open eyes, tapestry needle, stuffing

Rnd 1. 6 sc into MR (6)

Rnd 2. 6 inc (12)

Rnd 3. (sc, inc) x 6 times (18)

Rnd 4. (2 sc, inc) x 6 times (24)

Rnd 5. (3 sc, inc) x 6 times (30)

Rnd 6. (4 sc, inc) x 6 times (36)

Rnd 7. (5 sc, inc) x 6 times (42)

Rnd 8-18. 42 sc. Stuff firmly with polyester fiberfill as you work.

Rnd 19. (19 sc. dec) x 2 times (40)

Rnd 20. 40 sc

Rnd 21. (18 sc, dec) x 2 times (38)

Rnd 22. 38 sc

Fold in half, matching each stitch on the front with the next stitch on the back, working through both sides, sc in next 21 sts, secure end.

Ear tufts (make 2)

Wrap the yarn around your 4 fingers about 10-15 times, cut the yarn leaving quite a long tail. With that tail, wrap it 2-3 times exactly in the middle, dividing it in half, make a knot to secure it.

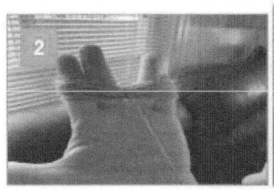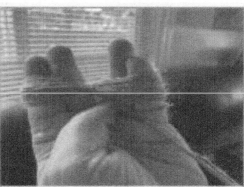

Cut double loops on the ends of the tuft in the middle to make them fluffy as shown in the picture. Using the same yarn tail, sew each tuft on both sides of the owl's head (on the ears).

Wings (make 2)

Use yellow yarn for the wings.
Rnd 1. 6 sc into MR (6)
Rnd 2. 6 inc (12)
Rnd 3. (sc, inc) x 6 times (18)
Rnd 4. (2 sc, inc) x 6 times (24)

Cut the yarn leaving enough length for sewing, secure the end, fold the wings in half and sew them to the body.
Beak (with the same yellow yarn).
Rnd 1. 4 sc into MR (4)
Rnd 2. (1 sc, inc) x 2 times (6)
Cut the yarn leaving the end to sew the beak to the head.

All done, congratulations!

CHAPTER 3 – TIPS AND TRICKS

Every crocheter requires tips and tricks to become a pro. The following tips and tricks make things easier when you begin crocheting:

Crocheting Using Thread

• When it comes to crocheting thread, remember that smaller is bigger. Threads are labeled according to their thickness. The thicker the thread, the smaller is the number. It is counterintuitive, but the more you crochet, the more you will get used to it.

• As a beginner, you can always start with a crochet thread 3, then move up to a 5 and 10. Size 20 or 30 threads can be used once you have built up your skills.

• As with the crochet threads, follow the same approach with steel crochet hooks. The smaller the size, the bigger the crochet hook. You can also look at the mm size that is usually printed on the hook itself. For example, a hook-sized 9 is 1.25 mm while the hook-sized 10 is 1.15 mm.

• As a beginner, you should start with a hook size that the pattern calls for. Once you have honed your skills a little more, you can adjust your hooks based on your comfort level and gauge.

• For beginners, it is always good to use steel crochet hooks. These hooks are much easier to use when it comes to working with thread.

• People often find crocheting using thread more difficult compared to using yarn, and it is only because of the thinner hooks involved. When you are working with the thread, all you need to do is choose a hook that has a bigger handle, that's all!

• When purchasing thread, always buy crochet thread and steer clear of embroidery or sewing thread. Although you can crochet with almost anything that resembles yarn or thread, you can make your life easier by sticking to the kind of thread that is meant for crocheting.

• When you work with yarn overs, make sure to work closely with the crochet hook head. You always want to ensure that the work on the hook is done above the segment of the hook, where it starts to get wider. Otherwise, your loops will be extremely loose.

• Another tip would be to thread around your non-crocheting hand, so it is easier to control your tension. This is extremely helpful when thread crocheting.

Crocheting Hacks with Yarn

• To prevent the balls of yarn from falling and rolling away while you are crocheting, put them in a hand wipe container. Just make sure to wash and clean it first. The yarn can be pulled through the hole of the hand wipe container.

• Use bobby pins or safety pins, or even a paper clip to mark your rows, or stitch a colored yarn or thread into the valley of the first stitch. Bobby pins and paper clips can be pulled out later once you are done.

• Use pencil boxes or jewelry boxes, or even a toothbrush holder to store your hooks.

• Use Excel sheets to map out your patterns. This is a great way to keep track of where you left off when your crocheting gets interrupted. You can also make the pattern larger to decrease eye strain.

• If you are worried about purchasing too much colored yarn that you won't be using in the future, just buy white washable yarn and dye it according to the pattern's colors.

• To keep your project in place, use yarn needles instead of hooks to weave the ends back through. This holds the project better and eliminates the chances of the yarn traveling.

• Instead of ironing your projects, which is not always ideal, mix water and starch in equal parts and spray liberally on your project; leave to dry on a flat surface.

• Keeping an index card with the lists of hooks and yarns you have is a great way to keep inventory. This ensures that the next time you are short of crochet supplies, you already know what you need.

• Yarns and other unfinished projects can be kept in zipper bags.
• It is always a good idea to keep foldable sewing scissors so that they don't snag in your crocheting bag.

• When in doubt, sew more tightly with string than you would with yarn. Try not to stitch so firmly that you hurt your hands. Knit somewhat more firmly than normal (except if you're now a skilled crocheter, at that point, simply do what you generally do!).

• Pay attention to the steps you're about to follow before you figure with thread crochet. Jumping from an acceptable hook size, worked with a cumbersome yarn all the way down to thread crochet, can make your thread paintings appear unbearably tiny. Steadily work your way down to the smaller sizes.

• Always do your crochet work in a good light so that you don't strain your eyes. This also makes crocheting easier. This is the same reason why, as beginners, you need to work with a lighter-colored thread as it makes it easier for you to find those little stitches.

• Crocheting is fun! Sure, it does have its own challenges, but that's only something you'll need to overcome at the beginning. Learning takes time, so be patient with yourself and enjoy each project you work on.

• Always choose beginner patterns when you're starting. This will make it easier for you to learn how to combine stitches and learn the ropes of crocheting.

• Working with a simple crochet swatch that uses basic stitches is always ideal, just to get the best results, minus the pressure of going through with a pattern.

CONCLUSION

Thank you for reading this book! Now that you have learned the basics of Amigurumi crocheting, it is time to incorporate them into the art of amigurumi. Starting with the basics is the usual thing that people do when learning a new craft or skill.

In crocheting and amigurumi, you could do various things like a cute dog or a lovely doll. However, you have to acquire a good foundation in order to do a great project. In amigurumi, learning basic crocheting is fundamental and essential.

You need to learn how to make a slip knot as it is the primary step to starting your work. After which, you could already work on various crochet stitches required for your work. It is important that you learn how to crochet through the front, back, or both loops. If you are working on the round, you should also know how to keep track of the completed stitches as well as mark the end of the round.

Crochet can be simple or as complex as you make it. In fact, as you get more and more experienced at crocheting, you will enjoy challenging yourself to create more and more projects. Creating Amigurumi crochet items is a great way of relaxing and will become second nature to you. As you practice and practice again using the images relating to the use of the crochet hook, you will soon find that this is something that you love to do and you'll work without even looking at what you are doing. It's that easy.

Amigurumi crochet is a practical and easy hobby, you can put it in your pocket and take it anywhere with you because crochet allows you to carry on your work in a moment of pause, at the bus stop, waiting for your children to come out of the school or gym, while waiting for public transportation, you can get on, sit, and pull everything out to keep working.

Besides, it is a therapy, great for soothing a tired and stressed-out mind and also it's a relaxing way to express your creativity and fill your life with colors.

As you work on a piece, for a while, you can forget your frustrations of the day and channel your mind into your work. Amigurumi Crochet is so relaxing that you will get completely lost in your new creation. When you finish for the day, your mind is refreshed. Thank you and good luck!

Printed in Great Britain
by Amazon

37097979R00073

A Transport Travel
by road, rail and water

Part 6: Wales, Man and Scotland

Cedric Greenwood

First published in 2018

British Library Cataloguing in Publication Data

A catalogue record for this book is available from the British Library.

ISBN 978 1 85794 500 3

Silver Link Publishing Ltd
The Trundle
Ringstead Road
Great Addington
Kettering
Northants NN14 4BW

Tel/Fax: 01536 330588
email: sales@nostalgiacollection.com
Website: www.nostalgiacollection.com

Printed and bound in the Czech Republic

Some of the pictures in this book appeared previously in the same author's Echoes of Steam and Vintage Voltage (Silver Link Publishing, 2015).

Acknowledgements

My thanks for making this series of books possible go to those who printed my black and white photographs: Ian Breckin of Silvertone, Leeds; Steve Howe of the Black & White Picture Place, Chester; and the late Ken Tyhurst of Canterbury.

Thanks also to those who processed my colour slides and prints: Fujifilm laboratories, Warwick; and CC Imaging Photo Lab, Leeds.

In writing the introductory text and captions I am indebted to the following people for information and assistance: Lewis Baron of the Douglas Bay Horse Tramway; Ted Gadsby of Walsall, Omnibus Society

librarian; Pat Rudrum of Holt, Norfolk, my Internet intermediary; Catherine Spiller, assistant collections curator, Dumfries Museum; Joy Thomas, Wrexham Local Studies librarian; and Tom Turner of Wallasey for help in identifying and dating of motor vehicles.

I am also indebted for information to the staff of the BAE shipyard at Govan; Manx Electric Railway, Douglas; Mitchell Library, Glasgow; and Norfolk County Libraries, for computer services at Holt.

Title page: **MANX ELECTRIC RAILWAY** The original car No 1 on the MER is pictured running southbound between Eskadale and Halfway House in unlined crimson and white with a crossbench trailer on 18 June 1964. It was the first of three cars of this type built by G. F. Milnes at Birkenhead for the opening of the line from Douglas to Groudle Glen in 1893. Their original Milnes bogies were replaced by Brush bogies in 1902. Car No 3 was destroyed in the Laxey car shed fire in 1930, but the surviving cars Nos 1 and 2 are the oldest electric railway or tramway cars still in public service anywhere in the world. For many years they were used as work cars with ladders slung under their rocker panels, but since the centenary of the railway in 1993 they have been restored for passenger service in smart, Victorian-style, lined-out paintwork and lettering.

Right: **HITCH-HIKING** was a common means of travel in the 1950s and '60s. Here, Miss Ruth Amos, from Margate, is a passenger in a 1957 Morris Commercial lorry at a fuel station on the A74 Carlisle-Glasgow trunk road in Lanarkshire on 21 May 1959. The fish merchant's lorry, on its way back home to Fife, took us exactly 100 miles from Kendal to Abington on our way that day from Skipton to Glasgow, part of a hitch-hiking and youth-hostelling holiday tour of Britain. In the background is a War Department railway 0-4-0 diesel shunter on a Pickford's low-loader.

Contents

Introduction

The final stage of our transport odyssey takes us on a course due north over the rugged western side of Britain, the Celtic fringe from Cambria to Caledonia, using the Isle of Man as a stepping stone on the way. On this final stretch we feature the three most fascinating tramways of all: the Mumbles Railway, the Manx Electric and Glasgow.

The largest tramcars in Britain ran on the oldest passenger railway in the world, the 5½-mile line around the eastern shores of the Gower peninsula. The **Swansea & Mumbles Railway** was a short line with a long and complicated history. Like many Welsh lines, it was built to carry minerals and diversified to carry passengers, who eventually became its only traffic. The line opened in 1806 as the Oystermouth Tramroad, an L-section plateway for horses to haul waggons of Mumbles marble and iron ore to Swansea and the docks; a branch from Black Pill served the Clyne valley coal mines. In 1807 a stagecoach was adapted to run on the line to carry passengers from Swansea to the beaches, and this is thought to be the world's first railway passenger service.

The passenger service was discontinued after the turnpike road opened in 1826. The railway was relaid in 1855 for steam mineral trains, and passenger services resumed in 1860, still with horses, now pulling open crossbench tramcars and converted railway carriages with steps up to more seats on the roof! Steam passenger trains ran from 1877 to 1929 with a tram engine and saddle-tank railway engines pulling passengers in a mixture of open wagons, carriages and double-deck, open-top tramcars – interspersed with through horse trams from the Swansea town system, which had running

powers till 1896. The Oystermouth Tramroad became the Swansea & Mumbles Railway in 1893, when the line was again relaid and now extended to Southend. It was further extended to Mumbles Head in 1898 when the new Mumbles Railway & Pier Company opened the pier as a passenger attraction. The diversity of rolling stock continued till 1929.

In 1927 South Wales Transport, the local bus company, took a lease of the railway and, surprisingly, electrified the line at 650 volts DC with automatic colour-light block signalling and reopened it in 1929 with 106-seat, 150hp double-deck tramcars, sometimes operating coupled together as two-car multiple units to carry the crowds at busy holiday times. As the cars ran beside the shore and sea wall most of the way, they had doors and vestibules on the inland side only as all the stations and halts were on that side of the line. It was a single line with passing loops and the automatic signals were set by the car pantographs touching signalling circuits in the overhead electric wires.

Not surprisingly, however, in 1958 the bus company bought out the railway company to substitute buses, and the line had to be cut back to Southend on 12 October 1959 to build a motor road for the buses along the cliffside tramway reservation to Mumbles Pier. The line from Swansea to Southend closed on 5 January 1960.

Wales is a land of quaint, narrow-gauge railways, which inspired Rowland Emett's railway fantasia in his cartoons in *Punch* magazine in 1939-53 and the working railway he built for the Festival of Britain funfair in Battersea Park in 1951. The Welsh narrow-gauge railways were usually built to carry slate from the mountains to the seaports in Merioneth and

Caernarvonshire, but this trade declined and buses and cars ate into the passenger traffic in the 1930s, leaving only the mineral traffic, mostly slate, to continue. The railways closed but some were taken over, rebuilt and revived in the 1950s by volunteers who still run them today as tourist attractions.

Emett was once photographed driving an engine on the **Talyllyn Railway**, a 2ft 3in-gauge line running 6½ miles from Towyn to Abergynolwyn in Merioneth. This is the only Welsh narrow-gauge railway that never closed, although it operated only two or three days a week, services were suspended for locomotive repairs, and the line had closed for the winter. Sir Haydn Jones, MP for Merioneth from 1911 to 1945, owned and managed the railway from 1911 until he died in 1950 at the age of 87. The Talyllyn then became the first railway in the world to be taken over by volunteers, who maintained its continuous operation in the summer of 1946 while restoring the track and rolling stock in the winter.

They found the track, two locomotives, four carriages, the stations and operations unchanged since the railway opened to slate in 1865 and to passengers in 1866, although the closure of the quarries in 1946 had put an end to mixed passenger and slate trains. The railway operated with only one engine in steam, hand-set points, no signalling, no telephone, no telegraph, no lighting and no heating. Beyond Towyn terminus the guard's van served as a mobile ticket office.

The railway was like a rural footpath with two slender rails and dished joints. In fact it was a rural footpath, not one marked on the map but a distinct trail, worn by local people, sheep and cows, between the rails in the otherwise grass-covered trackbed.

SWANSEA The Mumbles Railway ran along the seaward side of Oystermouth Road for most of the way and entered Swansea sandwiched between the road and the ex-London & North Western Railway (off right) that led to Swansea Victoria station and the docks. In this view, taken from the top of a tram, Swansea Bay No 2 signal cabin is on the right and the Bay View Hotel on the left. Both railways have now gone and Oystermouth Road has been widened across both trackbeds, but the Bay View Hotel survives on the corner of St Helen's Road (left).

From Towyn Wharf station on the coast, the railway runs inland, at first between high field hedges, then through a natural tunnel of trees at the edge of a hanging wood along the steep south side of the Afon Fathew valley. The train hobbled along the uncertain track at a top speed of 10mph.

Abergynolwyn terminus was 3 miles short of Talyllyn, the lake from which the railway takes its name. The extension to the Bryn Eglwys quarries gave access to a cable incline down to the village of Abergynolwyn in the valley below, where waggon turntables led to sidings serving the coal yard, the smithy, the writing

slate factory, the houses, the school and the chapel – a thorough service to the community!

The two original engines of 1865, *Talyllyn* and *Dolgoch*, and the four original carriages and brake van of 1866, have been restored and are still in service today. Part of the quarry extension beyond Abergynolwyn station has been reopened for passenger trains. The charm of the Welsh narrow gauge can also be experienced today on the Welshpool & Llanfair Light Railway, the Vale of Rheidol Railway from Aberystwyth to Devil's Bridge, the Ffestiniog Railway from Blaenau Ffestiniog to Portmadoc, and the Welsh Highland Railway from Portmadoc to Caernarvon (period spellings).

People visit these railways as a foil to the modern world, but the exigencies of health and safety regulations, tourists' needs for car parks, cafés and toilets and the way tourists dress these days tend to dilute the essential quaintness that attracted the preservationists and Rowland Emett in the first place, but it is good to see these railways in such a good physical and fiscal state after all these years.

Even the standard-gauge railways of Wales were rather quaint and had some station names I think would have appealed to Emett, such as Dingestow, Elms Bridge Halt, Ferndale, Mountain Ash, Mumbles Road, Nottage Halt, Quakers Yard, Six Bells Halt, Taff's Well, Upper Boat Halt, Welsh Hook Halt and Wolf's Castle Halt. These were all in the southern counties of Monmouthshire, Glamorgan and Pembrokeshire.

Wrexham was the centre of the north Wales coal and iron mines with a labyrinth of steeply graded, standard-gauge mineral and passenger railways serving the mining villages south and north of the town around Rhosllanerchrugog and Brymbo – areas also of Welsh male voice choirs. Wrexham was also the southern terminus of the Wrexham, Mold & Connah's Quay Railway serving Flintshire collieries and brickworks and shipping at Connah's

ABERGYNOLWYN This was the charm of the Welsh narrow gauge. Here we see the disused line of the 2ft 3in-gauge Talyllyn Railway beyond the passenger terminus to Bryn Eglwys slate quarries on 13 May 1960. The slate quarries were abandoned in 1946 but in 1976 the Towyn-Abergynolwyn passenger route was extended over part of the disused quarry line for 1 mile to Nant Gwernol.

Introduction

Quay on the Dee estuary. This railway became part of an anomalous enclave of the LNER, with Great Central stations and ex-GCR and LNER locomotives and carriages, well inside the territory of the GWR and LMSR.

How did the LNER, which otherwise served eastern Britain, arrive in Wales? The Manchester, Sheffield & Lincolnshire Railway teamed up with the Great Northern Railway and the Midland Railway to drive the joint Cheshire Lines from Manchester to Chester and Liverpool across the heartland of the London & North Western Railway. From Chester the MSLR independently headed west, joined up with the Wrexham, Mold & Connah's Quay Railway at Hawarden Bridge and together (as the joint North Wales & Liverpool Railway) they pushed on through mid-Wirral to Bidston by 1896 with running powers over the Wirral Railway from Bidston to Seacombe, giving freight access to Birkenhead docks, and passenger connection by Seacombe ferry to Liverpool. The MSLR bought the ailing WMCQR in 1897 and changed its own name to the Great Central Railway in 1899. The GCR became part of the LNER in 1923 while the LNWR and Wirral Railway were absorbed by the LMSR. In 1938 the LMSR handed over passenger service on the Seacombe branch entirely to the LNER.

The Wrexham/Chester/Seacombe triad of lines passed to BR's Midland Region in 1948 and saw some infiltration by ex-LNWR and LMSR locomotives. Passenger services ran from Wrexham Central to Chester Northgate and to Seacombe & Egremont with short workings from the three terminals to Shotton steel works. All trains stopped at all stations and halts; in 1950 the 30-mile journey from Wrexham to Seacombe, with 18 intermediate stops, took 1hr 25min, an average speed of just over 20mph. Caergwrle Castle, with its 13th-century ruins on a hill, was the object of excursions from Seacombe.

The Seacombe branch closed to passengers in 1960, when services were dieselised with multiple unit trains and diverted to New Brighton. A new service ran between New Brighton and Chester till the Chester leg closed in 1968. All trains from Wrexham Central now terminate at Bidston, connecting with electric trains to and from Liverpool. (The Seacombe end of this triad of lines is featured in Part 3 of this travelogue.)

From north Wales we hop over to the **Isle of Man**, right in the middle of the British Isles. In mid-century you could get there by the Isle of Man Steam Packet Company's classic, handsome, turbine passenger steamers built from 1927 to 1955 plying from Liverpool, Fleetwood, Dublin, Belfast and Ardrossan, which landed at Douglas harbour. There you met a horse tram and could set out on a complete tour of the island by quaint, veteran, 3-foot-gauge tramways and railways – horse, steam, electric and petrol.

I have been on holiday on the Isle of Man 11 times so far: twice in 1961, twice in 1964, once in 1967 during the period under review, and six times since between 1982 and 2005. **Douglas horse trams** are now unique in Britain. It's fascinating to sit on the front bench beside the driver to watch the muscular draught horse start the tram from each stop and, once in motion, the ease with which it trots along at a measured pace and instinctively knows where the next stop is – and when it's due to go off duty back to the stables. Watching the horse is a measure of how much easier it is to move a vehicle with steel wheels on steel rails than on an asphalt road.

Horsecar No 18 is a remarkable survivor: it's an open-top double-decker of 1883, which was the sole car on a 1-mile line from Broadstairs to St Peter's on the Isle of Thanet. The company failed financially and the tramcar was sold to South Shields in 1884 and sold on to Douglas in 1887.

The **Isle of Man Railway** was 47 route miles of 3-foot-gauge until the closure of the Peel and Ramsey lines in 1968, and had all the charm of the Welsh narrow-gauge plus the fact that this was a commercial, year-round service, not run by volunteers. The surviving Douglas-Port Erin line, 15½ miles long, is now nationalised by the Manx Government and runs from April to October only. The carriages date from 1881 to 1926, the derelict station at Santon has been reopened, a quaint little stop has been added at Ballabeg with a grass platform, and there is now an MER museum at Port Erin terminus.

I wrote in my travel diary on 17 August 1967:

'Douglas station was a haven of peace after the busy traffic in the streets of Douglas. There were eight or nine lines of carriages in the platforms and sidings and three shiny green locomotives coaling up and raising steam outside the sheds. Locomotive No 10, G. H. Wood of 1905, backed on to our train for Castletown and, although it was running late, which was normal on the IMR, the train stopped for unnecessarily long periods in the intermediate stations at Port Soderick and Ballasalla while the guard chatted to the driver, which also seemed normal practice.'

The trains with their elderly engines and archaic, wooden carriages moved at a cracking pace – quicker than on the Welsh narrow gauge – and rocked and clattered along the winding, overgrown, single track through fields and woods and forgotten-looking stations, stampeding the cattle and sheep grazing in the fields as if they had never seen a train before. Well, they don't see any trains outside the holiday season.

The horse trams and the steam trains were a bonus to me because I always went to the Isle of Man primarily to walk, ride, photograph, tape record and film the **Manx Electric Railway**, which survives in its original condition as created in the pioneer days of electric traction and is now the only line in the world that resembles the pioneer interurban electric railways of North America of the same period, the 1890s. America has nothing like it now.

Douglas Promenade horse tramway ends where the Manx Electric Railway begins its winding course along the east coast of the island to Ramsey. It's 11 miles from Douglas to Ramsey in a straight line, but the country is so hilly that the railway takes 18 miles to get there. This 3-foot-gauge line opened from Douglas to Groudle Glen in 1893, to Laxey in 1894 and to Ramsey in 1899. The 3ft 6in-gauge line from Laxey to the top of Snaefell opened in 1895.

This was all laid in double track and it was amazing engineering progress over such distances and arduous territory, involving land reclamation between Derby Castle and Onchan Head, viaducts at Groudle, Laxey, Ballaglass and Ballure, and a deep cutting at Ballagorry. There was no public electricity supply in the Isle of Man in the 1890s, so the MER built the island's first power station at its car sheds and workshops behind Derby Castle and powered not only the railway but also the Derby Castle entertainment complex, the Douglas Bay Hotel on Onchan Head and the first electric street lighting in Britain! The MER later replaced its Douglas power station with two others along the line at Laxey and Ballaglass. It was 1935 before the MER took power from the island's public supply, with sub-stations now at Douglas, Laxey and Ballagorry.

The MER was developed by the Isle of Man Tramways & Electric Power Company, which bought the Douglas horse tramway to extend the electric line to Victoria Pier and also constructed the 2-mile Upper Douglas Cable Tramway from Victoria Street, which operated from 1896 to 1929. On the liquidation of the IMTEP Company

in 1900 the MER Company took over the electric line and Douglas Corporation took over the horse and cable tramways. In 1906 the MER offered to lease and electrify the horse tramway but Douglas Corporation and the Isle of Man Government would not agree to it, so the MER has never reached its ultimate goal, Victoria Pier, nor realised its practical and commercial potential. The Government's proposal to close the horse tramway or to realign it on the seaward side reopens that possibility for a practical electric railway serving the main resorts of the island, but so far the island Government, which now owns both the horse and electric lines, is undecided.

Like many North American interurbans, the Manx Electric had its origins in real estate development at Howstrake, between Onchan and Groudle, and carried mail and freight too. It carried granite and setts from two lineside quarries, livestock, milk churns, corn, fertiliser, coal and general merchandise in wagons and vans drawn by a trolley locomotive, by the 'winter saloon' cars, by crossbench trolleycars, and in mixed passenger and freight trains. The railway also conveyed locked mailbags between Douglas and Ramsey and on certain trains the conductor with a bunch of keys collected the mail from eight lineside postboxes to hand over to the Royal Mail at Derby Castle.

The freight collection and delivery service ended in 1966 but the MER still has railway vans to carry merchandise and parcels from station to station when required. It lost the mail contract in 1975, when the Laxey-Ramsey section closed for two years and the Douglas-Laxey section closed for the winter of 1976-77.

Today the MER is a replica – a quaint, Manx, narrow-gauge, original, living replica – of those pioneer North American interurbans of the 1890s with its winding, roadside and cross-country route, its wayside stops, the style of its crossbench trolley

and trailer cars, and its saloon trolleycars with their clerestory roofs, arched windows, long wheelbases, cowcatchers and big headlamps.

In the 1960s the railway also still retained a late-Victorian atmosphere and charm with its rustic, wooden kiosks and seats at Douglas and Laxey stations, the faded blue photographs of the line in the waiting room at Laxey, the tall, globular lamps on the DC circuit at Laxey and Ramsey stations, and the station nameboard at Garwick Glen: 'for the beach, smugglers' caves and tea garden.' (Garwick Glen station has since closed.)

The Isle of Man does not enjoy such large crowds of visitors as it did in the first half of the 20th century and as a result of declining patronage the fortunes of both the IMR and the MER reached their lowest point in the 1960s and '70s. They have since recovered with the help of the Isle of Man Government, but now the Manx Electric Railway, like the horse tramway and the steam railway, no longer operates a winter service, running only from March to November. All three lines, horse, steam and electric, are now nationalised and subsidised by the Isle of Man Government.

Above all, the MER takes visitors through what

DHOON GLEN This is a typical Manx Electric Railway landscape, in Dhoon Glen on the 1899 extension from Laxey to Ramsey. Following the contours of the land as far as possible, the line loops around the glens along the way. In this picture on 17 August 1961 the double track crosses the bottom of the picture with one rusty traction pole and one new pole supporting the overhead electric wires. Past Dhoon Glen station (off left) it recrosses the picture between the hedgerows in the background, and a southbound two-car train can be seen approaching in the distance in the upper background of the picture.

I think is the most scenic part of the island. Most visitors change at Laxey to the Snaefell line, which climbs into bleak moors with cold winds and low cloud often blotting out the view, but to me the MER main line between Laxey and Ramsey is more scenic and interesting, leaving the road and winding through beautiful, rich green countryside, past the great cloud-capped hills and through wooded glens with wide views of the sea from high elevations, rising to 588 feet above sea level between Bulgham Bay and Dhoon Glen.

The Snaefell line, nevertheless, was a heroic engineering achievement, like the MER. It took the construction team only seven months to cut the 4½-mile roadbed out of the fellside on a ruling gradient of 1 in 12, to lay the 3ft 6in-gauge double track, erect the overhead poles and wires, and to build the power station halfway up the mountain with four massive boilers supplying steam to five engines driving the dynamos. Work began in late January 1895, was delayed by blizzards and thick snow in February, and the line was ready for opening on 21 August! The six cars were built by Milnes at Birkenhead in the same period.

From Snaefell summit the Isle of Man is spread out like a map below you and on a clear day you can see the dim outlines of England, Wales, Ireland and Scotland on the distant horizon, specifically the uplands of Cumberland, Caernarvonshire, County Down and Kirkcudbrightshire. Scotland is Man's nearest neighbour, only 17 miles from Point of Ayre to Burrow Head in Wigtownshire.

Scotland is our next and ultimate destination on this pictorial transport travelogue of Britain. Our Scottish narrative begins in Hamilton, Lanarkshire, on 21 May 1959. Ruth and I were **hitch-hiking** from Skipton to Glasgow on a youth-hostelling holiday. My travel diary reads:

'We thumbed the many big lorries that lumber

through this town on their way from England to Glasgow. I usually read the place names of the haulage companies on the cab doors. A Wigan lorry passed by ... and a few minutes later a man walked up to us and asked us where we were going. He was the Wigan driver of that lorry. He was going to Glasgow too and we walked with him to his lorry, parked about 200 yards up the street, climbed into the cab and set off on the last lift of that day's journey.

I told him we wanted to be set down at the outer terminus of the tramway to ride a tramcar into the city. He said he would be glad when the trams were taken off the road because it usually took him an hour to drive the 9 miles through Glasgow as it was impossible and illegal to pass the trams at stops, with their passengers walking across the road, and the tramcars accelerated and moved too quickly to be overtaken between stops. He added, though, that if he were a passenger he would rather travel by tram than bus. We first saw Glasgow's tramlines in the granite paved road at Uddingston, 7½ miles from Glasgow, but we saw no trams for the next 3 miles until, suddenly, a fantastic, antique, gaunt-looking, standard Glasgow tram came rocking and lurching around the bend ahead and whined past on the other side of the road. Then followed another and another and so on, some standard cars and some semi-streamlined, late-1930s "Coronation" cars, all to some vague, rural terminus named Broomhouse at which the former line to Uddingston had been curtailed in 1948, by municipal pedantry, within the city boundary.

We got out of the lorry at a tram request stop ("Cars stop here if required") and waited for one of those standard trams to return from Broomhouse. At first only the "Coronation" cars returned but we didn't flag them. Some of them slowed for us and some even stopped but we ignored them. Their crews looked mildly surprised when they passed

because there was only one route out here and all the trams were going the same way. Even Ruth did not want to go in a modern tramcar when there were museum-piece trams in the offing. We waited in the chill wind of the evening, walking in circles and to and fro and banging our arms to keep warm. Eventually the standard trams reappeared, grotesque, bobbing along, but they were only going 1½ miles to Parkhead depot. The crews made comic gestures about the size of our rucksacks and the pots and pans hanging off them, and when, after 20 minutes, a city-bound standard tram came along and we flagged it and climbed aboard, the motorman walked through the lower saloon to intercept us on the conductor's platform. He exclaimed at our luggage and told us in no uncertain manner that we ought to wait for a more modern tram but that he would take us in this one if we were willing to risk it!

We mounted the narrow, curving staircase with a brass handrail, opened the sliding door to the upper saloon, with its dark, varnished woodwork, and, peering through the tall, soot-stained windows, we entered **Glasgow** in traditional style along Gallowgate, a long gloomy corridor of soot-black, featureless, four-storey, stone tenements through the east end of the city. From the windows of the tenements, wind-tousled heads – the "window hangers'" of summer days – watched the tramcars go by (there was little other traffic). From the windows of the tramcars the passengers looked out on a succession of grim side streets of more tenements, the golden balls of the pawnbrokers, Red Hackle whisky billboards, men sitting – some asleep – on the sidewalks outside the bars and half-clothed children playing in the streets.'

On my first visit to Glasgow, in August 1956, I arrived at St Enoch station on a 'Starlight Special' from St Pancras and found myself in Tramtopia. The city was veritably milling with gaunt old tramcars.

Double-line convoys of them nodded and rocked along, clanking through junctions and lurching around corners. They were going to fantastic-sounding destinations, writ large on the worn, torn and soot-stained roller blinds in those mahogany boxes on the ends of the cars: AUCHENSHUGGLE, BATTLEFIELD, CAMBUSLANG, EGLINTON TOLL, FERGUSLIE MILLS, GALLOWGATE, MILNGAVIE, POLLOKSHIELDS, ROUKEN GLEN and YOKER.

Although a few rural sections had closed, the sprawling Glasgow system was still mainly intact. This was the year before the closure of the Paisley lines and two years before the city council decided to close the rest of the system. More than 900 cars were still operating out of 11 depots on more than 100 miles of route when other British cities had only a few lines left. Unfortunately I had no time to explore the system; I rode a standard tram on line 8 from Renfield Street to Millerston and hitch-hiked north to join friends hosting me at Aviemore.

Glasgow tramways were an anachronistic fantasy to anyone from south of the border. On my second visit, with Ruth, in 1959, here was a large city system that was still virtually complete when all other tramways in Britain had closed or were on their last legs – and here, once more, we could still ride on Liverpool bogie streamliners banished from their native city five to six years earlier. The canyons of four- and five-storey tenements of grey and red sandstone seemed to be a suitable theatrical backcloth designed specifically for the old standard four-wheel and bogie trams of the period 1900-28, which blended with their environment like wild animals in their habitat. As I learned during multiple visits over the next and last three years of the system, 1960-62, a tramcar journey through Glasgow was a series of human encounters not experienced elsewhere and I found the tramway men in Glasgow were more friendly and accommodating than anywhere else.

GLASGOW CROSS station on the underground steam railway is on the right of this photograph of Trongate with a 1951 'Cunarder' car and two pre-war 'Coronation' cars on 1 June 1962. The policeman in a white coat is on 'point duty' regulating traffic at the junction with Saltmarket (left). The red sandstone station was on the Caledonian Railway's 3-mile cut-and-cover tunnel under the main streets from Dalmarnock Road to Stobcross Street. The Glasgow Central Line, as it was called, closed in 1964 and reopened in 1979 as the electric Argyle Line with a new station a quarter of a mile west in Argyle Street, leaving an uneven spacing of stations between Bridgeton Cross and Glasgow Central. Glasgow Cross station was not demolished till 1977; its site is now a triangular, paved pedestrian island in the east fork of Trongate.

The tramway system reached its peak in 1948 with 1,207 cars operating out of 11 depots along 135 miles of double track, extending through neighbouring burghs and rural reaches east to Airdrie, south to Clarkston, west to Elderslie and north to Milngavie. For years after other big cities had scrapped the trams, Glasgow's streets still echoed to the ring of steel on steel, the eerie drone of electric traction motors and the hiss of bow collectors on the overhead wires.

The Corporation's own workshops at Pollokshields built the tramcars of steel, teak, mahogany, deal and rock elm and many cars were 60 years old by the demise of the system. These older cars had started life as open-toppers with trolleypoles and were gradually upgraded over the years with central upper saloons, enclosed platforms, enclosed balconies, upholstered leather seats, longer-wheelbase trucks, more powerful motors, air brakes and bow collectors, all of which prolonged their active life. Now up to 60 years old, their interiors were like a museum of Edwardian woodwork and brasswork with inlaid patterns in the varnished wooden ceiling of the lower saloon and carved lintels over the doors. There was a smell of leather seats and of soot inlaid by decades of working in a smoky, industrial city. Traction motors groaned under the floorboards and woodwork creaked as the cars rocked along with a gentle, nautical, pitching motion. They had amazingly powerful acceleration and braking and were reputed to be capable of 60mph. They and the modern 'Coronation' and 'Cunarder' bogie cars of 1937-54, with their restrained streamlining and Art Deco saloons, gave a much smoother, quieter and more civilised ride than the motorbuses that replaced them.

The Corporation scrapped the trams in the five years 1957 to 1962, starting with the lines beyond the city boundary, but Glasgow, more than any other British city, seemed reluctant to part with its tramcars after surviving all others in Britain except the Blackpool-Fleetwood line that still runs today.

The city had five 'last cars' spanning a period of 13 days. The last regular service car ran on the night of 1/2 September 1962 amid a great crowd from Yoker to Bridgeton Cross bearing the enthusiasts' headboard 'The end of the greatest British tramway'. Then, for the next three days, 'for those who wish to make a last tram journey', the Corporation ran a special short working of service 9 between Anderston Cross and Auchenshuggle with eight cars supplementing the replacing buses from noon till 10.00pm on 2 and 3 September and from noon till 5.30pm on 4 September. Crowds estimated at 250,000 then lined the route to watch the funeral procession of 20 tramcars, dating from 1894 to 1951, headed by restored cars for the transport museum, wend its way from Dalmarnock depot to Pollokshields works, arriving at 7.30pm. The last car, 'Cunarder' 1379 of 1951, was thought to be the official last tram. Then the Burgh of Clydebank wanted its 'last car', so 'Coronation' 1282 of 1940 was wheeled out to carry the Provost and a civic party on a round trip from the Town Hall to Dalmuir West, Yoker and back on the evening of 6 September. That was the official last tram to run in Glasgow and is now kept in working order at the National Tramway Museum in Derbyshire.

Few people saw the last trams to run in Glasgow: 62 cars left in Dalmarnock depot ran in ghostly convoys every night in the small hours of 11-15 September through the city centre to Pollokshields workshops for disposal, the last being 'Coronation' 1165 of 1938. Glasgow kept more of its retired tramcars than any other British city – six cars representing the period 1894-1938 – which are the nucleus of the Glasgow Museum of Transport collection. A seventh car, a 'Cunarder', joined the collection after the break-up of the British Transport collection at Clapham, London. More Glasgow trams are preserved than those of any other British system: a total of 20 at static and working museums, including six standard cars and six 'Coronations'.

North of Glasgow and the central lowland industrial belt of Scotland, roads lead into **the Grampian Mountains and the North West Highlands**, where, in the 1950s, there was relatively light motor traffic and most A class roads were still single track with passing places, marked by white diamond road signs; some A roads in the North West Highlands are still like this today. Most Scottish drivers, who were used to the mutual give-and-take on these narrow roads, were considerate and patient, and even the English drivers, by the time they had penetrated this far north, had become mellowed, cautious and respectful. Also, in those days there were no ferries across the sea lochs or to the islands in western Scotland on Sundays.

On 22 May 1959 Ruth and I were passengers in a lorry that took us from Dalmuir West tram terminus for 25½ miles to Tarbet on the A82 to Fort William. Only 18 miles by road from Glasgow Cross, we were rolling along the narrow, winding road that followed almost every indentation and promontory of the heavily wooded 'bonny banks of Loch Lomond' with distracting glimpses of the view across the loch, when suddenly, as my travel diary describes

'...we were confronted by a lordly ram, with a narrow, black face, long horns describing circles around its ears and overloaded almost down to the ground with potential knitting. It was standing, statuesque and solemn, in the middle of the road half facing us. It stood its ground, unmoved by fright or even courtesy, and ignored the lorry. Luckily the ram was standing abreast of a passing place on the road by which we managed to circumnavigate it and it still stood like a statue until it was out of sight behind us. Fortunately there was very little other traffic on the A82 even alongside such a celebrated beauty spot as

Loch Lomond, so near Glasgow, in the middle of a perfect summer Saturday.'

We hitch-hiked on from Tarbet to Tyndrum, where we stopped for a picnic in

'...the silence of mountain solitude in the western nook of Perthshire, a silence broken only by the occasional passing car, a distant goods train looking like an OO scale model on the mountainside and the whistle signals of a shepherd to his sheepdog.'

Our next driver was on his way from Glasgow to Fort William for the weekend. He was a middle-aged Glaswegian with a big chin, an upright, noble bearing, a gentle and unruffled manner and a soft, slow, deliberate speech like a Hebridean. He drove in an easy, gentle and cautious manner and took us 46 miles right to our destination at Glen Nevis youth hostel and treated us to a generous high tea at the Bridge of Orchy Hotel on the way. In Glencoe we stopped at the village Post Office to stock up and stretch our legs. I bought our driver a packet of cigarettes and when Ruth observantly noticed he smoked. He had been shopping too and when he came back from his walk he gave Ruth a booklet of photographs of Glencoe and I gave him the cigarettes. We laughed and set off again in the car.

The A82 crossed Loch Leven, the boundary between Argyllshire and Inverness-shire, by the quaint Ballachulish ferry, a small, motorised float named *Appin Chief* with a swivelling platform for four cars and a drawbridge at each end.

'We chugged gently through the swirling, bottle green waters of the loch with a marvellous view west of two ships anchored in the wide, deep, placid waters, cradled by steeply shelving mountains.'

The only alternative to the ferry on Sundays was an 18-mile detour around the head of the loch. The ferry was replaced by a road bridge in 1975. Most ferries in western Scotland now run a service on Sundays.

The **A830**, the only **road to Mallaig,** runs west from Fort William to Arisaig then north along the western seaboard to Mallaig on the north-west corner of the Morar peninsula. This is the last reach of the traditional 'Road to the Isles' that comes 'by Tummel and Loch Rannoch and Lochaber' in the words of the song. Motor traffic is shipped from Mallaig to 'the small isles' and to Skye. I shall let my travel diary of 23 May 1959 take us to the end of our travelogue:

'The car that brought us down Glen Nevis turned along the A82 to Inverness and dropped us at a lone signpost pointing west and bearing just the name: MALLAIG. A remarkable-looking iron bridge with castellated portals over the River Lochy was an appropriately dramatic entrance to the road to Mallaig and somehow signified the speciality of what lay ahead. The first mile, across Corpach Moss to Banavie, is the transition from the ancient, grim Grampian Mountains across the floor of the great rift valley to the younger, rugged North West Highlands. We waited in blazing, hot sunshine for one and a half hours for the next lift; very few cars came along this road and they were either local or fully occupied. Eventually a quiet, middle-aged couple from Herefordshire took us all the 44 fantastic, breathtaking, memorable miles to Mallaig.

The massive, surly bulk of Ben Nevis appeared to rise in sombre majesty ever higher as we left it behind and proceeded along the north shore of Loch Eil. From Loch Eil all the way to Mallaig the road weaves a fantastic course through an apparently impassable tract of mountains, ravines, waterfalls, forests and lakes. The road is only about 10 feet wide with vague lay-bys for passing places and it lurches, dips and bends so much that there are many sudden corners and hillbrows where drivers cannot see the road more than about six yards ahead. This, it seemed to me, was Britain's Khyber Pass and, oddly enough, there is a hamlet called Khyber just beyond Mallaig. There were, of course, the additional hazards of vehicles, including occasional buses and lorries, coming in the opposite direction and sheep crossing the road. Sheep make a point of waiting till a vehicle gets near them and then cross the road in front of it. The maximum, average, safe speed to drive along this road is 15mph but it is worth driving slowly to see some of the most beautiful country in Britain. The road takes a more intimate part in the landscape and affords much better views than the railway, which is in cuttings and tunnels for much of the way.

We passed through Glenfinnan with its tall monument to Bonnie Prince Charlie at the head of the fjord-like sea Loch Shiel, like a Victorian gilt-framed painting of the Highlands with cows standing in the water's edge. The 11 miles from Glenfinnan to Kinlochailort is the most fantastic and arduous section of the road to Mallaig and the civil engineering works that were moderating the corners, gradients and hillbrows with cuttings, embankments and new bridges added to the hazards of the drive with their equipment of bulldozers, lorries, tar boilers and steamrollers, which we had to pass with extreme care.

From the snug, verdant glens between Loch Eil and Loch Eilt we continued west into the stern desolation of rough, craggy, rolling moors with low, brooding mountains at the seaward end of the Morar peninsula. I had read that the road between Kinlochailort and Arisaig was rebuilt in 1938 but I should not have suspected it otherwise. Down at Arisaig, a scattered village of small, rough, whitewashed cottages on the Atlantic coast, we had our first view of "the small isles", the plateau of Eigg and the rugged outline of Rum boldly commanding the horizon. The famous white sands of Morar stretch along the west coast of the peninsula from Arisaig almost to Mallaig. The hamlet of Morar is situated on a heavily wooded inlet, where the waters of Loch Morar, the deepest loch in Scotland at 1,017 feet, issue down gradual falls into the sea.

Thence it is a short way to **Mallaig**, a herring fishing village and a port for mail steamships to Skye and the Outer Hebrides. It is a scattered, unrelated collection of hard-faced, rugged, grey stone cottages and villas on a north-facing headland of bare, craggy rock washed by a deep, transparent, green sea. The A830 entered the village down a short, steep, main street and ended in a jumble of fishing boats on the beach in the harbour. There is a strong reek of fish and the whole place echoes to the eternal cries of seabirds. Four and a half miles across the Sound of Sleat the mountainous isle of Skye, the most romantic of all the British Isles, fills the horizon to the north-west, so near and yet so far. We learned that we had missed the last ferry to Skye and, as no public transport operates in western Scotland on Sunday, that was the last ferry till Monday. We decided to relax, eat and bask on the rocks and return to Glen Nevis hostel.

It was lunch time on Saturday, the fishing fleet was in for the weekend, there were no train arrivals or departures for the next three hours and Mallaig was inactive and dormant in the blazing hot sunshine. The scene was so peaceful that almost every movement could be heard distinctly: the creaking of oars in rowlocks, the soft, sing-song voices of fishermen mending their nets, repainting their boats or just standing on the pier with their hands in their pockets, and the occasional hum of a motorcar on the road around Mallaig bay.

The railway from Fort William approaches Mallaig through cuttings in the towering granite cliff by the sea. We had to cross the railway to get to

the shore and, as we were doing so, the signalman leaned out of his high cabin and told us that we should find a more pleasant and secluded part of the shore if we walked south along the railway for a few hundred yards! It was unusual for us, from highly civilised and electrified south east England, to be told by a railwayman to walk along the railway, but it was typical of the humanity and friendliness of people in such remote parts. We could see other people walking along the railway as casually as if it were a public footpath and it did not matter because there were no stock movements at Mallaig for the next three hours.

Towards five o'clock we returned along the railway to the village and saw ahead of us, on the rails between which we were walking, a locomotive standing and steaming at the head of a train in the station. There was little or no road traffic leaving Mallaig so we decided to go by train back to Fort William. The locomotive was ex-Great Northern "K2" Class 2-6-0 *Loch Laing*, built in 1918, characteristic of the locomotives that work this line. It laboured with its train of maroon carriages, humming lowly and creaking, along the single track, which was skilfully engineered and winds unobtrusively through the beautiful but obstructive landscape.

The iron road to Mallaig was the last addition to the national railway system, being built by the North British Railway between 1897 and 1901 as an extension of the West Highland Line from Glasgow. It was notable for the use of reinforced concrete for the construction of the viaducts and tunnels, which have weathered to look like stone. It runs in close company with the road, the A830, with which it plays a continual game of cat-and-mouse, crossing and re-crossing, underneath and overhead, hiding behind hills and running along the opposite shores of the lochs. We halted at small stations with sturdy buildings providing ample shelter from wet

and windy weather. The platforms were adorned by well-kept flower beds and rockeries, rustic fencing and oil lamps. From the carriage window at Corpach station we had a fine view of Ben Nevis from across Loch Linnhe. In the foreground of our view was the wheelhouse and funnel of a "puffer" – one of the small tramp steamers that ply between Glasgow and the Hebrides – peeping above the edge of the lock at the south end of the Caledonian Canal.'

I regret that I cannot find the negative or print of the photograph I took of that view.

I imagine that there is no longer any sense of adventure in driving through the West Highlands of Scotland and that the road to Mallaig has lost its romance and the sense of achievement it gave to 'keep right on to the end of the road'. Most of the A class roads have been rebuilt as wide, two-lane carriageways with much improved visibility and no sudden hazards, which is just as well in view of the trend to mass motoring after 1960. There is now a car ferry from Mallaig to Armadale on Skye and even a high-level road bridge to Skye from Kyle of Lochalsh, otherwise the landscapes and seascapes remain unspoilt. I have not been back to Mallaig since; on previous experience elsewhere I think I prefer to remember it as it was. I hear it is quite a busy place with special tourist trains and gift shops, and I see that there are now nine car ferries a day to Skye and six on Sunday. At least we could have reached Skye on Saturday afternoon if we'd had a service like that in 1959 – and we should not have had to walk 7 miles along the railway by Loch Carron when we found Stromе Ferry closed for the Sabbath on the following day's journey to Achnashellach youth hotel in Ross & Cromarty (there was no motor road along the east coast of Loch Carron in those days).

Ugly diesel locomotives now growl through the glens, but steam-hauled tourist trains are integrated with the regular diesel service on the line from Fort

William to Mallaig, although you have to pay a premium for the privilege.

I also prefer to remember Glasgow as it was with its heavy industries, tenements, ubiquitous tramcars and torpid Sabbath rather than the city of unemployed, urban deserts, pedestrian zones, one-way streets and frenetic Sunday trading.

Two days after our pilgrimage to Mallaig, on 25 May I experienced my most successful venture in hitch-hiking. My diary recalls:

'The first vehicle that crossed Strome ferry was a large, luxurious, streamlined brake, which cruised leisurely and quietly up the narrow and otherwise empty road in the smiling morning sunlight and stopped for us outside Achnashellach youth hostel. Our hosts were a husband and wife, exiles from London now living in Kenya but taking their holidays in Britain for cheapness, seeing Scotland for the first time and being pleasantly surprised at what they missed when they were living in Britain. They treated us to tea and biscuits in the large, handsome, baronial hotel at Achnasheen before we branched onto the tortuous A832 past some of the most ancient mountains on Earth and around the wild sea coast by Gairloch and Gruinard Bay. They took us all the 96 miles on our intended, devious itinerary that day and dropped us outside the youth hostel at Ullapool, the "ultima thule" of that 1959 expedition.'

GLASGOW and HIGHLAND ROYAL MAIL SERVICES

Telegraphic Address. MACBRAYNE, GLASGOW. Telephone: CENTRAL 9231

PLEASE REFER TO AC/IBT

DAVID MACBRAYNE LIMITED
CLYDE HOUSE,
44 ROBERTSON STREET,
GLASGOW, c.2.

David MacBrayne's comprehensive and integrated network of passenger, mail and freight services by steamship, bus and lorry were vital to the isolated communities of the western highlands and islands. The ramification of routes extended from Glasgow and Campbeltown to Inverness and Stornoway. The name of David MacBrayne and the emblem in silhouette of a highland warrior with his sword held aloft on the sides of the buses and lorries are held in hallowed memory and are almost part of the mythology of the highlands and islands.

In 1878 David MacBrayne, a partner in David Hutcheson's shipping company of Glasgow, succeeded to the ownership of the company and inaugurated the large, fast and comfortable Royal Mail PS *Columba* on the Glasgow-Ardrishaig run and soon developed services to more than 100 ports of call in the west and north of Scotland. David MacBrayne Jnr took over the firm in 1902 and MacBrayne's buses began to meet the ferries in 1906, also carrying mail and parcels. In 1928 MacBrayne's lorries extended the freight network with scheduled runs on routes connecting with the ferries. The 'buses' were all single-deck coaches, mainly Maudslays, Bedfords and AECs with coachwork in bright red, cream and light green. They were short, lightweight vehicles for the

torturous highland and island roads.

The David MacBrayne identity continued under Coast Lines and LMS Railway joint ownership from 1928 till nationalisation. In 1969 the bus routes were apportioned to the Scottish Bus Group companies Highland, Western and Alexander Midland and to Hebridean independent operators. In 1973 the ferries passed to British Rail's Caledonian Steam Packet Company and in 1985 the road haulage services were sold to Kildonan Transport of Turriff, Aberdeenshire. The name MacBrayne lives on in the Caledonian MacBrayne car ferries, large and small, plying everywhere between Ardrossan and Stornoway.

I took an interest in MacBrayne's transport empire from 1952, when I was 14 and living in Kent, and I obtained their literature and timetables but I have no photographs of MacBrayne's vessels or vehicles because their ferry and bus schedules were sparse with only one or two trips a day. I was never in the right place at the right time.

Glamorgan

Glamorgan

17

Left: **MUMBLES** Pier was the outer terminus of the Swansea & Mumbles Railway, which ran 5½ miles around the shores of Swansea Bay. Here, on 2 August 1959, we see one of the double-deck tramcars dating from electrification in 1929. The line was electrified at 650 volts DC with double overhead wires to feed the 120hp motors of the big cars running at high speed, sometimes as two-car multiple units. The 278-yard-long pier was opened in 1898 and, after periodic closures for restoration, remains open today with a lifeboat station in place of the former landing stage and visitor amenities at the pier entrance.

Right: **MUMBLES** This is the interior of the upper saloon of Swansea & Mumbles car No 10 at Mumbles Pier on 2 August 1959. These 45-feet-long double-deckers were the largest tramcars in Britain, with 106 seats. They were double-ended, so the seats, which were upholstered in leather, were reversible as on normal tramcars.

A Transport Travelogue by road, rail and water, 1948-1972

Left: **MUMBLES** Car No 10 of 1929 rocks along the 1898 extension of the Mumbles Railway from Southend to Mumbles Pier on the same day. The town of Oystermouth in the distance was the original terminus of the line, opened in 1807 as the horse-drawn Oystermouth Tramroad. The extension had to be cut out of the cliffside of Mumbles Head and was retained by a sea wall. The cars had doors on the inland side only as all the stations and halts were on that side of the line. The centre rails, laid along most of the single-line sections, were bonded to the running rails to increase the negative return current to the power station.

Two months after this photograph was taken this section of the line closed for conversion to a motor road for buses to take over the entire route five months later.

Above: **WEST CROSS** In this view from a Mumbles tramcar, Swansea-bound, we see West Cross Halt, where the line ran close to the high-tide mark with a low sea wall around the shores of Swansea Bay. A cycle path now follows the track of the railway from Swansea to Mumbles.

Glamorgan

Left: **SWANSEA** terminus of the Mumbles Railway was at the town end of Oystermouth Road. On 2 August 1959 we see car No 10 again, one of the 106-seat, 120hp electric cars built by the Brush Electrical Engineering Company in 1928-29, when the former steam railway was electrified. Sometimes they ran coupled together as two-car multiple unit trains to carry the crowds at busy periods. The line from Swansea to Southend closed on 5 January 1960.

Below and overleaf: **SWANSEA** Rutland Street car shed housed the fleet of 13 electric cars at the Swansea terminus of the Mumbles Railway. These huge Brush bogie cars were painted crimson and cream.

Denbighshire

MARFORD Abandoned, rusty and forgotten, this 0-6-0 saddle tank engine, bereft of builders' plates and nameplates, was a relic of a standard-gauge industrial railway at the disused Rossett Sand & Gravels quarry. The engine could be seen at close quarters from the GWR main line between Wrexham and Chester and was standing on parallel exchange sidings buried in sand. The quarry was situated at Springfield Lane, Marford, near Rossett, where a spur off the main line between Gresford and Rossett stations led to four sidings of GWR and LMSR trucks, shunted by the quarry company locomotive. Rossett Sand & Gravels Ltd opened this quarry in 1927 initially to supply sand for concreting the Mersey road tunnel. This 0-6-0 inside-cylinder saddle-tank engine, *Netherton*, built in 1903 by Manning Wardle at Leeds, was bought second-hand from the construction contractors Sir Lindsey Parkinson & Company at Winwick Quay, Warrington, in 1943. The sand quarry closed in 1948 and *Netherton* was scrapped a few months after this photograph was taken in 1952, when the quarry was reopened by the United Gravel Company, using lorries to remove the mountain of sand. The quarry closed in 1971 and this is now a Site of Special Scientific Interest owned by the North Wales Wildlife Trust.

A Transport Travelogue by road, rail and water, 1948-1972

CEFN-Y-BEDD was a rustic station on the former Great Central/LNER triad of lines from Wrexham Central to Chester Northgate and Seacombe ferry, which divided at Hawarden Bridge. The view is looking south towards Wrexham on 10 July 1958. These ex-GCR stations, with their brick buildings, gardens and oil lanterns, are now unstaffed halts with new shelters and electric lights. The station had no footbridge and passengers crossed the line to the opposite platform by the timber barrow crossing in the foreground.

CAERGWRLE CASTLE & WELLS was another station on the Wrexham leg of the triad of GCR/LNER lines to Chester and Seacombe via Hawarden Bridge. A locomotive and goods brake van pause outside the signal cabin during shunting on the daily pick-up goods duty. Trains to Seacombe ferry were diverted to New Brighton in 1960 and now terminate at Bidston, connecting with electric trains to Liverpool. The Chester leg of the triad closed in 1968, and today Caergwrle station has lost its suffix 'Castle & Wells'.

AFON WEN Two coaches from Merseyside on a day excursion to Snowdonia are parked outside the Pwllgwyn Hotel on the A541 road between Mold and Denbigh in August 1951. A day trip by coach was the highlight of the year for those who could not afford to spend all their fortnight's holidays in a seaside resort or holiday camp. Coach hotels such as this were licensed to open in the mornings to cater for outward-bound coach parties taking their mid-morning break. These coaches, owned by Harding's of Birkenhead, are in a tasteful colour scheme of grey trimmed with smoky blue. The leading coach is a 1947 Burlingham-bodied Leyland and the rear coach looks like a 1938 Harrington-bodied Leyland. In those days all coaches carried the company name, address and telephone number in stylish signwriting on the back (now they show only the Internet web address in sans-serif, lower-case, adhesive vinyl lettering).

Harding's coach company dated from 1891 when Alfred Harding began running horse-drawn waggonettes and removals from a depot and office at Charing Cross, Birkenhead. The family-owned company was taken over by a Liverpool firm in the 1970s, the name continued but the coaches were white and the name disappeared in a take-over by Selwyn's Coaches of Runcorn in 2006.

Left: **LIVERPOOL-DOUGLAS** Liverpool -bound Isle of Man turbine steamer *Lady of Mann*, built by Vickers Armstrong at Barrow in 1930, is seen over the stern of the Douglas-bound TS *Manxman* (Cammell Laird, Birkenhead, 1955) as they cross halfway on the Irish Sea passage on 19 September 1964.

Right: **DOUGLAS** Gulls circle overhead as the Isle of Man turbine steamship *Ben-my-Chree*, built by Cammell Laird at Birkenhead in 1927, loads at King Edward VIII Pier, Douglas, for Liverpool on 20 June 1964. The *Ben-my-Chree* was the progenitor of 11 passenger ships of this design built for the Isle of Man Steam Packet Company until 1955. Three of them were lost in the evacuation of Dunkirk in 1940 and replaced after the war. These handsome vessels, looking like small Cunard liners, began to be replaced by car ferries from 1962, and the *Ben* was retired from service in 1965. The Steam Packet Company operated motor vessels from 1972 and was taken over by Sea Containers Isle of Man in 1996.

A Transport Travelogue by road, rail and water, 1948-1972

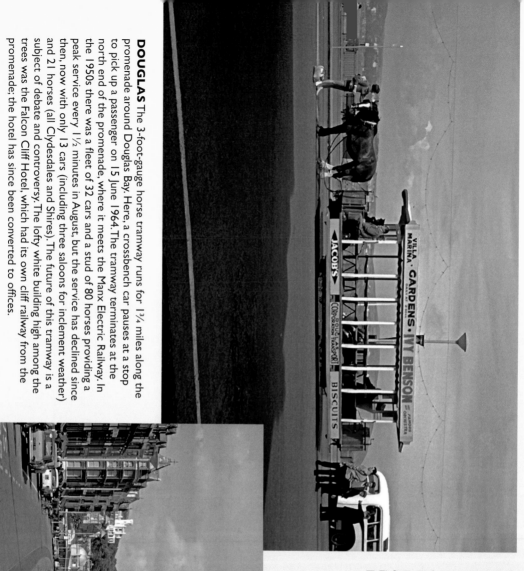

DOUGLAS The 3-foot-gauge horse tramway runs for 1¾ miles along the promenade around Douglas Bay. Here, a crossbench car pauses at a stop to pick up a passenger on 15 June 1964. The tramway terminates at the north end of the promenade, where it meets the Manx Electric Railway. In the 1950s there was a fleet of 32 cars and a stud of 80 horses providing a peak service every 1½ minutes in August, but the service has declined since then, now with only 13 cars (including three saloons for inclement weather) and 21 horses (all Clydesdales and Shires). The future of this tramway is a subject of debate and controversy. The lofty white building high among the trees was the Falcon Cliff Hotel, which had its own cliff railway from the promenade; the hotel has since been converted to offices.

DOUGLAS This profile of Douglas Corporation crossbench horse tram No 46 of 1908 at Victoria Pier terminus is set against the backdrop of Douglas Bay and Onchan Head on 9 June 1961. The tramway dates from 1876 and it has been the only horse tramway in the British Isles since the one at Fintona, County Tyrone, closed in 1957; those at Morecambe and Pwllheli ceased in 1926 and 1927. The service originally ran all year round, but since 1927, when the Corporation put buses on the promenade, the horse tramway has run only in the summer holiday season, currently from April to November.

DOUGLAS station, with its substantial, glazed redbrick buildings, four platforms and extensive canopies, was the central terminus of the Isle of Man Railway's three lines to Peel, Port Erin and Ramsey. On 7 June 1961 the Peel train in the station is headed by 2-4-0 tank engine No 11 *Fenella* of 1844, in the Indian red locomotive colour of the period 1944-65. The Isle of Man Railway Company, which operated mainly in summer with skeleton services in winter, closed down in 1965. The Marquis of Ailsa and friends leased and operated the three lines for the summers of 1967 and '68 but at great financial loss. The Peel and Ramsey lines then finally closed and the track was lifted. Lord Ailsa, now with a modest Government grant, continued to operate the Port Erin line in 1969-71, but still at a loss. The IMR Company, with a bigger Government grant, resumed operation of the Port Erin line in 1972. The railway was eventually nationalised by the Isle of Man Government in 1980 and the summer service still runs on the 15½-mile Douglas-Port Erin line today, the carriages now repainted in dark brown and white. Since the closure of the Peel and Ramsey lines, Douglas station has lost its canopies and half its platforms, which have been replaced, symbolically, by a bus depot and car park.

DOUGLAS Derby Castle is the name of the joint terminus where the Douglas promenade horse tramway meets the 550-volt Manx Electric Railway, on the same 3-foot gauge, for onward travel along the east coast of the island to Laxey and Ramsey, a journey of 17¾ miles. The horse trams terminated under the freestanding cast-iron canopy in the background, demolished in 1980. On 9 June 1961 the electric train in the foreground – trolleycar, crossbench trailer and 6-ton van – dates entirely from 1899, built throughout by G. F. Milnes & Co at Birkenhead, as was most of the stock on the line. Derby Castle was the name of a castellated hotel with a dance hall and variety theatre, later replaced by the intrusive, concrete Summerland leisure centre, which was demolished after a fire. The joint tram terminus is still called Derby Castle today. Many generations of the Earls of Derby held office as Lords of Man on behalf of the British Crown from 1405 to 1736.

GROUDLE GLEN The Manx Electric Railway (MER) is a roadside and cross-country interurban line winding around the headlands, hills and wooded glens along the east coast of the island. Here, trolleycar No 20 tows a crossbench trailer car up the 1 in 24 gradient out of Groudle Glen southbound to Douglas on 18 June 1964. Car 20 is one of four 'winter saloons' that were built by Milnes for the Laxey-Ramsey extension in 1899 and provide the basic service. The original Milnes bogies on cars Nos 19 to 22 were replaced in 1904 by J. G. Brill bogies from Philadelphia to give a better-quality ride.

GROUDLE GLEN The 2-foot-gauge Groudle Glen Railway, built in 1896, runs for three-quarters of a mile through the wooded glen and along the clifftop high above the sea. Two Bagnall 2-4-0 tank engines, *Sea Lion* of 1896 and *Polar Bear* of 1906, were named after the menagerie of animals enclosed in the sea-washed coves, once viewed from footbridges beyond the terminus. The polar bears were released in 1914 and the sea lions in 1939, when the railway closed for the two world wars. In the 1940s metal thieves and vandals postponed post-war reopening till 1950, with *Polar Bear* only. Saboteurs again put the railway out of action from 1959 to 1961, when it reopened for two seasons. A green *Polar Bear* is seen here with a train arriving at the glen terminus on 17 August 1961 with its train of crossbench coaches built in 1896-1905 by G. F Milnes at Birkenhead, the same firm that built cars for the MER during the same period. Vandal havoc closed the railway again after the 1962 season and the two engines went to England.

The railway was restored for reopening in 1986. The locomotive *Sea Lion* is back in its original light green paintwork, supplemented by other restored narrow-gauge engines. *Polar Bear* is now working at Amberley Chalkpits Museum in Sussex. The original Milnes coaches have been rebuilt and accompany both engines at Groudle Glen and Amberley.

A Transport Travelogue by road, rail and water, 1948-1972

ESKADALE North of Groudle Glen the railway runs alongside the country road to Baldrine. Here we see trolleycar No 5 of 1894 towing winter saloon trailer car No 59 southbound on 16 June 1964. Six of these trolleycars were built by Milnes for this extension of the line from Groudle Glen to Laxey and the start of the year-round service in 1894, and four of them survive today. Cars Nos 5, 6, 7 and 9 have recently been refitted with one-piece windscreens, which does nothing for their aesthetic appearance but allows the use of windscreen wipers. Trailer car No 59 is one of only two saloon trailers on the roster, built in 1904 by the Electric Railway & Tramway Carriage Company at Preston with an open platform or veranda at each end; they are rarely used in service.

HALFWAY HOUSE–BALDRINE Protected by the two-aspect highway signals, a crossbench trolleycar with a crossbench trailer crosses the Douglas-Ramsey main road southbound between Scarff's Crossing and Halfway House on 18 June 1964. It was a rare treat to ride on the front seat beside the motorman on these crossbench trolleycars but it could be breezy. There were no seats outside the bulkheads on the trailers. Car No 32, seen here, and sister car No 33 were built in 1906 by the United Electric Car Company at Preston on Brill bogies with General Electric motors, and were the two fastest cars in the MER fleet. There were originally nine crossbench trolleycars in the fleet by different makers dating from 1898 to 1906, but only five are still on the roster and usually only appear in service when traffic exceeds the capacity of all the other serviceable stock.

The overhead line equipment on the MER is unusual with centre poles and copper running wires suspended from brackets on each side, about 16 feet high (higher at road crossings) and aligned for fixed-head trolley wheels for more reliable high-speed operation. The steel poles are buried 5 feet in the ground and are more closely spaced on the curve here than on the straight line beyond. The rail joints are copper bonded to complete the electric circuit to the power substation.

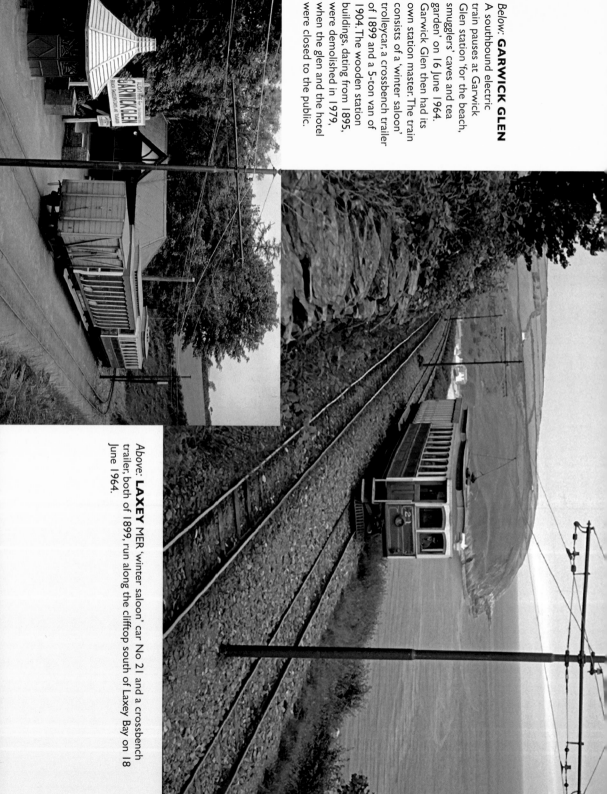

Below: GARWICK GLEN
A southbound electric train pauses at Garwick Glen station 'for the beach, smugglers' caves and tea garden' on 16 June 1964. Garwick Glen then had its own station master. The train consists of a 'winter saloon' trolleycar, a crossbench trailer of 1899 and a 5-ton van of 1904. The wooden station buildings, dating from 1895, were demolished in 1979, when the glen and the hotel were closed to the public.

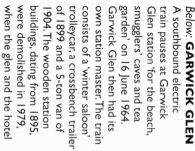

Above: **LAXEY** MER 'winter saloon' car No 21 and a crossbench trailer, both of 1899, run along the clifftop south of Laxey Bay on 18 June 1964.

LAXEY With Laxey Glen and Snaefell (2,034 feet) in the background, car No 22 of 1899 wakens the echoes as it drones up the 1 in 40 gradient along the south side of the glen towards South Cape with a crossbench trailer and van in tow on 18 June 1964. Laxey village nestles in the glen below. Car No 22 was rebuilt by Manx craftsmen with replica coachwork after an electrical fire in 1990, and re-entered service in 1992.

LAXEY station, with its rustic wooden buildings in a glade of cawing rooks, is seen on 16 June 1964 – and not a passenger in sight. The through line of the 3-foot-gauge MER is on the right and on the left is the lower terminus of the 3ft 6in-gauge Snaefell Mountain Railway. This 4½-mile line to the summit was built and electrified in seven months ready for opening in 1895, and the MER took it over in 1902. Snaefell cars Nos 1 and 6, seen here, are two of the fleet of six cars of 1895, again by Milnes of Birkenhead. In the centre MER car No 20 of 1899 pauses southbound from Ramsey to Douglas.

LAXEY Electric railway cars of two gauges meet here to exchange passengers for scenic journeys up Snaefell and along the coast to Douglas and Ramsey. Car No 4 on the left was one of six built in 1895 for the opening of the 3ft 6in-gauge Snaefell Mountain Railway, which starts here and runs 4½ miles up Laxey Glen on a ruling gradient of 1 in 12 to a terminus at 1,990 feet, just below the 2,034-foot summit viewpoint. The Snaefell cars picked up the overhead current with a bow collectors, one on each end of the car, instead of a trolley, to cope with high winds on the fells.

Car No 21 on the right was one of four built for the extension of the 3-foot-gauge Manx Electric Railway from here to Ramsey in 1899. The two types of car are pictured side by side on 17 August 1967 awaiting passengers for Snaefell and Douglas. Car No 21 sports an impressive array of front-end equipment: two electric headlamps, an oil marker lamp, a coupler and cowcatcher, together with the usual cornerwise steps for passengers boarding and for the conductor to serve the trailer car in transit.

Right: **LAXEY** The interior of MER Milnes car No 20 of 1899 on 16 June 1964. These cars have 48 upholstered, transverse, reversible seats in two saloons, originally for smokers and non-smokers, with a panelled wooden partition and a Tudor-arched pane in the door. Cars Nos 19 to 22 were built with wooden seats, which were replaced with upholstered seat cushions and backrests in 1932; they have since been reupholstered.

Below: **BALLASKEIG BEG** The great hills ranging from Snaefell (2,034 feet) to North Barrule (1,860 feet) form the backdrop to the Manx Electric Railway between Laxey and Ramsey, seen here with northbound trolleycar No 7 of 1894 towing a crossbench trailer car on 17 August 1961.

RAMSEY The only section of the MER that looks like a street tramway is this 100-yard section alongside Walpole Drive, which has side traction poles and was originally laid with grooved rail. When the line was built in 1899 the Ramsey Commissioners planned to pave the full width of Walpole Road incorporating the tramway, but the ballasted track still runs along a natural roadside reservation of compressed soil and stones and is only paved across side streets. In this picture car No 22 of 1899 has stopped to drop passengers at the corner of Queen's Drive on 17 June 1964. The line continues along a private right of way behind the houses on Waterloo Road to the terminal yard on Albert Street.

RAMSEY Trolley and trailer cars on the MER change places by power and by gravity at crossover points in the track at Douglas, Laxey and Ramsey stations, where trainsets reverse for return journeys. The ritual was recorded here at Ramsey terminus on 6 June 1961. Trolleycar No 22 has uncoupled from the trailer car, run forward on the down line and reversed over the crossover to the up line. The station master has released the handbrakes on the trailer car to run by gravity down the slope beyond the crossover. The conductor waits to turn the trolley pole around car No 22 to reverse over the crossover and back on to the trailer. Both these cars were built by Milnes at Birkenhead in 1899. Laxey station has two crossovers in the track for the reversal procedure there. The building on the left was the former Plaza cinema, named on the timetable as the Ramsey terminus.

RAMSEY Queen's Pier was built by the Isle of Man Harbour Board in 1881–86 for Irish Sea ferries calling here on their way between Douglas, Belfast and Ardrossan without the need to berth in the harbour. As the pier was 717 yards long – nearly half a mile – the 3-foot-gauge construction tramway was retained to carry passengers and luggage on hand trucks to and from the pier head. Here at the pier entrance on 17 June 1964 we see the 10-seat petrol tram of 1950, while in the siding is the 1937 diesel locomotive with a passenger coach and flatcars waiting for the next ship.

RAMSEY The 10-seat Wickham petrol tram of 1950 negotiates the passing loop halfway along Queen's Pier on the same day. The last ship called here in 1970, the tramway closed in 1981, and the pier closed in 1991. The derelict structure, which has lost its deck buildings and railings, is now under restoration.

Right: **RAMSEY** The Isle of Man Railway started the Isle of Man Road Services in 1930, when it bought out the two bus companies on the island and coordinated all bus services with the railway, with joint publicity and ticket availability. All the island's bus garages doubled as bus stations with waiting rooms and offices. This is Ramsey bus station on the corner of Queen's Pier Road and Prince's Road on 18 June 1964. The island bus services were worked entirely by single-deckers until 1946, and the three Leyland buses on the forecourt date from 1947. The two double-deck PD1s also had Leyland bodies, which were unusual in having odd ventilator windows at the front of the upper saloons.

Below: **RAMSEY** harbour was the home of the Ramsey Steamship Company, which carried bulk cargoes around the Irish Sea. At Ramsey it exported lead from Foxdale mines until 1960 and imported coal from Whitehaven, building materials and animal food. On 17 June 1964 the motor coaster *Ben Vooar* ('big mountain' in Manx), built in 1950, is berthed at the East Quay. Beyond it is the Market Place with St. Paul's parish church, and on the right is the West Quay with its agricultural merchants and ships' stores. The Isle of Man Railway, which served the lead mines, ran a harbour branch from Ramsey station via Derby Road and along the West Quay until 1954.

The Albert Tower on the hill in the background, Llergy Frissel, commemorates an informal visit to that spot by Queen Victoria's consort, Prince Albert, in 1847. The Royal Yacht anchored in the bay and the Prince went ashore early next morning for a walk. He asked the first man he met, the town's barber, to show him the way up the hill and the barber led him to the top. The Ramsey Steamship Company was 101 years old when it was wound up in 2014, but its ships, now with other companies, can still be seen in Ramsey and around the British Isles.

RAMSEY The afternoon train hobbles slowly through the grass and weeds along the uncertain track into the derelict-looking terminus station at the north end of the Isle of Man Railway system on 16 August 1967. This was the first summer of Lord Ailsa's era of operation after the whole system had been closed for one year. The locomotive, 2-4-0 tank engine No 11 *Maitland* of 1905, is in the green paintwork of the Ailsa era. The building alongside is the two-road carriage shed with timber walls and a corrugated-iron roof. The line in between led to the one-road, two-engine shed built of the local slaty stone. The Ramsey line was opened by the Manx Northern Railway in 1879, was amalgamated with the Isle of Man Railway in 1904, and finally closed at the end of the 1968 summer season.

A Transport Travelogue by road, rail and water, 1948-1972

KIRK MICHAEL On the indirect railway journey from Douglas via the west coast to Ramsey on 20 June 1964, 2-4-0 tank engine No 12 *Hutchinson* of 1908 takes time out to uncouple from its train, shunt these two coaches out of the down siding and add them to the front of the train. The handsome, rock-faced, red sandstone station building, off left, has been preserved as a private house.

RAMSEY Pictured outside the engine shed on 16 August 1967, No 11 *Maitland* is an example of the standard 2-4-0 tank engine built for the Isle of Man Railway by Beyer Peacock at Gorton foundry, Manchester, to a similar design built by that company for 3ft 6in-gauge railways in Norway. The green paint scheme of the Lord Ailsa era was a revival of the original IMR scheme carried from 1873 to 1939. Until 1954 the Ramsey train engine ran beyond the station and along Derby Road to shunt the harbour sidings during the terminal lay-over.

ST JOHN'S A summer idyll on the Isle of Man Railway on 20 June 1964: 2-4-0 tank engine No 5 *Mona* of 1874 simmers in the sunshine while the driver takes his lunch break in the stone-based signal cabin, built by the former Manx Northern Railway in 1879. This was the point where the 16½-mile MNR line to Ramsey joined the IMR line from Douglas to Peel. The signalman has left his lady's bicycle leaning against the ladder up the ex-MNR wooden, slotted-post, semaphore signal, which is the up main starter. When the line was clear the signal dropped vertically into the slot and the oil lamp on top of the post turned to show a green light. The water tank is on the left.

PEEL IMR 2-4-0 tank engine No 4 *Fenella* of 1884 and its two-coach train stand at Peel terminus alongside the harbour with the castle in the background on 7 June 1961. The 11½-mile line from Douglas to Peel was the first of the three lines of the IMR, opened in 1873 and closed in 1968. The station has been replaced by a car park. Only the 15½-mile line from Douglas to Port Erin, opened in 1874, survives today and there is an IMR museum in the old bus garage next to Port Erin station. The ruins of the 14th-century castle and the 13th-century cathedral beyond it within the castle bailey stand on St Patrick's Isle, connected to the mainland by a causeway that is an extension of the harbour west quay. The isle was the one-time seat of the Norse kings of Man and the Isles (including the Hebrides, Kintyre, Arran and Bute) from 1079 till 1263, when it passed to the Scottish crown. The Isle of Man later passed to the English crown. The Norse colonists of the island established the Tynwald, the Manx Parliament, which, dating from c977, is the oldest continuous parliament in the world.

Dumfries-shire

DUMFRIES Three red buses of the Western Scottish Motor Traction Company animate this High Street scene on 31 May 1962. The bus on the right is a Northern Counties-bodied Guy of 1945-46. The buses complement the ruddy-brown sandstone buildings, notably the Town House and Mid Steeple (1705-07) and the burgh church of St Bride (1868). The Victorian fountain celebrates the public water supply to Dumfries. On the facing wall of the Town House is a cast-iron plate of 1827 showing the stagecoach mileages to Annan, Castle Douglas, Carlisle, Edinburgh, Glasgow, Portpatrick, Huntingdon and London. The two buses on the left, advertising 'Shop at Binns', are loading outside Binns's emporium. Binns was a chain of large department stores, founded by George Binns at Sunderland in 1811, with many branches in towns from Middlesbrough to Edinburgh, and the bold 'Shop at Binns' advert was displayed on the front and back of buses in that area.

This lively picture of the town centre contrasts with the rundown scene today. High Street is now a pedestrian zone with fancy paving, terraced in places, and cluttered with all the street furniture imaginable. Most of the shops have changed ownership and uses,

although Burton the tailor still occupies the building on the right. The Binns buildings is now divided into small shops; today you can only 'shop at Binns' in Darlington.

EDINBURGH The concealed radiator was the new look of 1953, when this Edinburgh Corporation bus was built with a Metropolitan-Cammell 'Orion'-style body on a Leyland PD3 chassis. It was photographed at a stop on the ascent of Dundas Street, Edinburgh, on route 27 to Oxgangs on 15 April 1963. Oxgangs is an old measure of arable land.

Lanarkshire

Right: **UDDINGSTON** On this old cast-iron fingerpost in Glasgow Road on the A74 trunk road from Carlisle, photographed on 21 May 1959, a black hand in low relief points the way to Glasgow while the sign to Bothwell and Hamilton is a wooden board with hand-painted lettering. It stood at the junction with the A721 New Edinburgh Road. Solidly built dormer bungalows in red sandstone with parkland gardens overlooked this location, where Glasgow tramcars passed on their way to Main Street, Uddingston, until 1948, when line 29 was cut back to Broomhouse Zoo, the first of the Glasgow tramway closures.

The signpost has now gone and the bungalows are masked from view by a jungle of rhododendrons in the front gardens. The M74 motorway, which has eclipsed the A74 from Carlisle, crosses under Glasgow Road immediately south of this junction.

Left: **DALMARNOCK** A Glasgow Corporation 'Coronation' car of 1939 drones through the grim canyon of four-storey tenements, like a street through a prison; the streets are paved with granite setts the full width of the roadway. This is Dalmarnock Road at Davidson Street (right) on 8 March 1962, and the tramcar is on line 26 bound for Scotstoun via Partick. The 'Coronation' cars on EMB bogies from 1937 to 1941 and another six were built in 1954. All the buildings in this view have been cleared and the scene is now a semi-urban desert.

BRIDGETON A standard Glasgow tramcar stands out against standard Glasgow tenements on Dalmarnock Road on 27 May 1961. Car No 76, built by the Corporation on Brill trucks in 1920, has had its broken lifeguard tied up with string by the motorman in a city traffic jam after noisily dragging it over the granite setts from Argyle Street to Clydebank and back. The happy crew held up following tramcars for the photograph before reversing into Ruby Street and Dalmarnock depot for repair. These hexagonal-dash tramcars were built over the period from 1910 to 1924. Line 26 from Farme Cross to Clydebank was replaced by motorbuses on 2 June 1962.

BRIDGETON A Glasgow Corporation 'Cunarder' class tramcar of 1949 glides past the wide open plain of granite setts at the junction of Dalmarnock Road (left) and Old Dalmarnock Road (right) on line 26 from Farme Cross to Clydebank on 27 May 1961. Glasgow built 100 of these tramcars on Maley & Tauton bogies from 1948 to 1952 and they were nicknamed after the great Cunard ocean liners built by John Brown's shipyard at Clydebank.

The telephone kiosk on its island in the middle of the junction has a distinct lean to the left owing to subsidence. There are many pedestrians about but few motorcars, characteristic of a city of tenement dwellers; the car on the right is a 1939 Morris 8. Dalmarnock gas works dominates the background in Old Dalmarnock Road.

All the residential and industrial buildings in this picture have gone and been replaced with pleasant, modern housing only two or three storeys high. The forked road junction has been replaced by a landscaped, triangular green, making a T-junction of the two roads. Since the tramways closed in 1962 the durable granite sett-paved streets have been replaced by asphalt in a constant, execrable state of erosion with cracks, patches and potholes ever since, giving all road users a rough ride.

BRIDGETON Cross was a five-way tramway junction in the east end of Glasgow with London Road across the background. A 'Coronation' tramcar of 1939 is about to turn into Dalmarnock Road (right) on line 26 to Farme Cross on that same May day. Trolleybus overhead wires turn into James Street (left). The ornate cast-iron bandstand-like structure was built and donated by George Smith's Sun Foundry of Glasgow in 1875 to shelter the unemployed, and was called 'The Umbrella'. It was accompanied by a police telephone kiosk, a tramway inspector's kiosk and railed steps to underground lavatories. The domed corner building on the right is the Olympia cinema of 1911, part of the ABC circuit from 1924 till closure in 1974.

All the buildings in this picture still stand today, cleaned and restored, but all the shops have changed hands and half of them are now empty and shuttered. 'The Umbrella', then painted black, has been repainted in two-tone blue with white spandrels and gold details on the clock tower, but the public seats and lavatories have been removed. Bridgeton Cross today is not the busy community centre it was then and this viewpoint is now screened by trees.

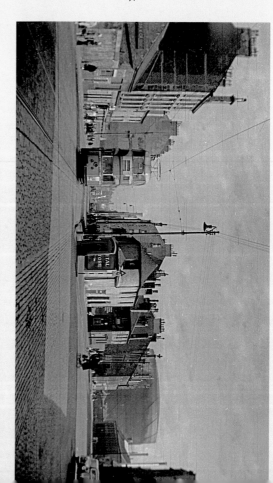

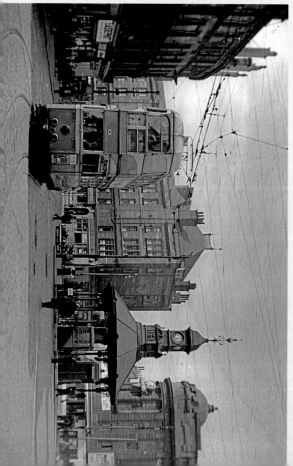

GOVANHILL Trolleybuses came to Glasgow in 1949, late in the trolleybus era, to begin replacing the tramcars. This was Britain's last and only post-war trolleybus installation (apart from the short Teesside extensions in 1951-68) and Glasgow was the only city in Scotland with trolleybuses except for Dundee's experiment with them in 1912-14. Only six trolleybus routes were installed in Glasgow, and from 1958 the Corporation began to replace tramcars with motorbuses instead. Consequently tramcars, trolleybuses and motorbuses were all running at the same time in Glasgow from 1949 to 1962 – and single-deck trolleybus routes added to the mixture. Then in 1965 the trolleybus routes began to be replaced by motorbuses too. This 1962 Crossley-bodied BUT trolleybus, No 123, is speeding along Aikenhead Road, Govanhill, on route 102 from Riddrie to Polmadie on 17 April 1966. The route closed later the same year and this trolleybus was the last to run in Glasgow, for a photo-call on 28 May, the day after the closure of trolleybus services.

GOVANHILL This 1958 Crossley-bodied BUT trolleybus is in Cathcart Road on 17 April 1966, and the two uniformed busmen on the right are a conductor and driver from the nearby Larkfield garage, which was shared by motorbuses and trolleybuses. This route, the 105, was the last trolleybus route in Glasgow, closing on 27 May 1967, and the quiet hum of electric traction, so appropriate to this empty Glasgow Sabbath scene, was replaced by diesel buses. Govanhill looks much the same today, but all the shops along Cathcart Road have changed and many have been closed and shuttered. The prominent barber's shop pole sign on the left has also disappeared.

CAMLACHIE A Coal merchant is seen riding his horse-drawn wagon in Campbellfield Street, off Gallowgate, on 26 May 1961. He is selling coal for 8s 6d a hundredweight (when there were 20 shillings in the pound). As a sign of inflation, 1 cwt, or 50kg, of coal today ranges in price between £15 and £20, depending on quality and where you buy it. Campbellfield Street disappeared in slum clearance about 1970 and is now the site of St Mungo's Academy.

CAMLACHIE Glasgow 'Coronation' car No 1155 of 1939 and a Central SMT all-Leyland low-bridge bus of 1948 are city bound along Gallowgate, also on 26 May 1961. The tramcar is on line 15 from Baillieston to Anderston Cross.

CALTON London Road, half a mile east of Glasgow Cross, is viewed from the top of a tramcar on 2 September 1962. Air brakes hiss as oncoming 'Coronation' car No 1243 of 1939 stops to pick up a passenger on its way to Auchenshuggle. Glasgow's official last service car had run the previous evening, but it looked like normal service for the next three days when the Corporation ran a special short working of line 9 between Anderston Cross and Auchenshuggle with eight cars running alongside the replacing buses for those who wished to take a last tram ride.

POLLOKSHIELDS Two Glasgow Corporation work cars are seen in Barrland Street permanent way yard on 1 September 1962. On the left is water tank car No 19, built in 1907, used for washing and brushing the tracks. On the right is welder car No 21, built in 1905 with a shortened body from an 1898 bogie single-deck passenger car remounted on an electrified horsecar truck. These cars were normally seen out on track work only at night when no trams were in service.

Below: **GLASGOW CROSS** Steam rises from the low-level railway station in this view of Trongate from a tramcar emerging from London Road on 21 December 1960. Pedestrians are clad in long overcoats and the white-coated policeman is on point duty where the single overhead wires for the trams crossed the double overhead wires for the trolleybuses passing between Saltmarket (left) and High Street (right). Ahead, a lightly laden lorry follows a Corporation 'Kilmarnock bogie' tramcar of 1927-28, almost in silhouette, on line 26 from Burnside to Scotstoun, about to converge with tramcars from Gallowgate. The two motorcars on the right are a 1956 Wolseley 680 and a 1960 Rover 90. Glasgow Cross station (right) occupied a triangular site in the middle of this five-way junction of main streets in the old city centre. The streets were still paved with granite setts across their full width, but have since been repaved with asphalt. All the overhead wires have gone and some of these shops have closed as the focal point of city life has moved west and Glasgow is no longer busy with through traffic.

GLASGOW Old tramcars built from 1900 to 1928 still haunted the streets of Glasgow and outnumbered the more modern cars throughout the city when this picture was taken in Argyle Street, the main axis of the tramway system, on 22 May 1959. The two four-wheel standard tramcars on the left are eastbound on line 29, Maryhill to Tollcross, although the leading car is on a short working to Glasgow Cross, where it will reverse. The private car sandwiched between them is a 1956 Morris Minor estate car with a timber frame at the back. Leading the line of oncoming tramcars is a 'Kilmarnock bogie' of 1928-29 on line 9 from Auchenshuggle to Dalmuir West.

The tramlines and granite setts have been replaced with asphalt and Argyle Street is no longer a through route for road traffic to Trongate, being blocked by a pedestrian precinct from Queen Street to Glassford Street. Most of the buildings in this picture are still there today with only a few glass-faced blocks merging unobtrusively into the building line and general elevation.

GLASGOW Two gaunt old standard tramcars on line 15 meet on Argyle Street on 22 May 1959. Car No 311 was built in 1909 and is westbound to Anderston Cross, while car No 927, of 1900, emerges from beneath Central station bridge, eastbound to Baillieston. Central station, terminus of the old Caledonian Railway, spans the street for 130 yards, and acts as a sounding board for the tramcars, echoing the ghostly drone of the electric motors, the sound of the wheels drumming over the rail joints and the hiss of the air brakes. At this crossroads just east of the station the two tramcars are about to hammer across the tracks linking Jamaica Street (left) with Union Street (right).

Since the electrification of the main line, Central station has been cleaned and attractively repainted with the name 'Central Station' in relief serif lettering across the lintel of the bridge, and advertising has been removed.

Above: **GLASGOW** On the west side of the bridge carrying Central station over Argyle Street an eastbound 'Cunarder' car pauses while a 'Coronation' car turns north into Hope Street on 27 May 1961.

Right: **GLASGOW** In the commercial heart of the city 'Coronation' car No 1194 of 1938 descends Hope Street, jangling through the trailing junction with the line from Bothwell Street (left) and passing the corner of Gordon Street by the Central Station Hotel (extreme right) on 27 May 1961. Hope Street rises up the north slope of Clydesdale in a series of terraces, levelling out at intersecting streets, drops across the defile of Sauchiehall Street, and rises again to Cowcaddens. A ride on a tramcar down this switchback was a fascinating experience.

This scene is substantially unchanged today. All the buildings have been cleaned, showing the ruddy brown sandstone facades. Hope Street is now one-way, uphill, for northbound buses, taxicabs and bicycles only. The wider street section in the foreground is now divided by parallel lines of railings marking off a cab lane on the right and a bus bay on the left.

Above: **GLASGOW** The Victorian Gothic pile of the Christian Institute and other buildings dwarf 1939 'Coronation' car No 1185 as it drifts down Bothwell Street on line 18A from Springburn to Shawfield on 26 May 1961. This service closed eight days later. The Christian Institute filled the block from West Campbell Street to Blythswood Street and was built in three sections by two architects in one unifying style: the Christian Institute (John McLeod, 1878-79), the Bible Training Institute, and the Young Men's Christian Association (R. A. Bryden, 1895-98). The YMCA was a 189-bed hostel and restaurant providing lodgings at reasonable prices for young men working in the city.

Owing to rising maintenance costs and new fire regulations the building was demolished in 1980 and replaced by a soaring glass skyscraper. The rest of Bothwell Street and the west side of the city centre has been transformed with many modern, high-rise office blocks.

Left: **GLASGOW** On its way from Scotstoun West via Great Western Road, standard tramcar No 95 of 1923 passes through Sauchiehall Street, Glasgow's main shopping street, destined for Dennistoun in the east end on 22 May 1959. Wellington Street is on the left. This section of Sauchiehall Street is now a pedestrian precinct and the buildings on the left have been replaced by a modern shopping complex called the Sauchiehall Centre.

Lanarkshire

COWCADDENS A frequent service of cars on line 29 to Maryhill is seen at the top of Hope Street in the Cowcaddens district of Glasgow on 27 May 1961, only five months before the closure of this service and 14 months before the last tram in the city. The 29 was then the only tram service operating up this end of Hope Street, where the cars turned left into Cowcaddens Street, which terminates the view. 'The Cowcaddens Equitable Loan' is signwritten across the first floor of the building in the background.

ANDERSTON There are six Glasgow tramcars in this picture of Anderston Cross on 25 May 1961, three on lines 9 and 26 along Argyle Street (right) and three on the double-track stub sidings in Stobcross Street (left), the terminus of line 15 from Baillieston. It seemed as if Glasgow trams would roll on forever, but line 15 closed in March 1962 and line 9, Glasgow's last tram service, from Auchenshuggle to Dalmuir West, was cut back to Anderston Cross (Stobcross Street) on 2 September; the last car ran from here on the 4th. The two-storey building on the curve into Stobcross Street is Anderston Cross station on the steam underground railway from Dalmarnock to Finnieston, designed by local architect John Burnet for the Caledonian Railway. The station closed in 1959 and the train service ceased in 1964. Anderston Cross was the centre of this township, which was a separate burgh from 1824 to 1846. The stone cross that once stood here was called the 'stob' and Stobcross Street once led to Stobcross House, the mansion of the Anderson family. The town that grew here became Andersonstown, which evolved into Anderston. Stobcross House was demolished to make way for Queen's Dock.

The entire town centre was wiped out by a

massive road junction with slip roads and footbridges, completed in 1971, as seen here from the same viewpoint and looking in the same direction on 30 June 2012. Here, the M8 motorway on a concrete viaduct crosses the Clydeside Expressway that flattened Stobcross Street and replaced the westward continuation of Argyle Street, which has been blocked by new housing between here and Finnieston. The photograph was taken when the Clydeside Expressway was clear of the normal streams of traffic to show the complete environment. Down a hole under this concrete jungle is a new railway station, now named only Anderston, on the central low-level line that was reopened in 1979 as part of Glasgow's extensive suburban electric railway system, and which now enjoys the highest percentage patronage of the local population of any British city. Queen's Dock, which replaced Stobcross House, was closed to shipping in 1970 and partly filled in for car parking.

POSSILPARK Glasgow 'Coronation' car No 1170 of 1939, on line 18, passes the gates of Macfarlane's Saracen Foundry in Hawthorn Street on 27 May 1961, seven days before the line closed. Line 18 crossed the city from Burnside in the south-east to Ruchill in the north-west, then turned east across the north of the city via Possilpark to Springburn. The tower of Ruchill Hospital can be seen in the background. The junction in the overhead wires here marks the turnout into Saracen Street on the former line 27 from Springburn to Shieldhall, closed in 1958.

Scotland was the home of ornamental iron foundries, Glasgow was the capital of the industry, and Macfarlane's was the largest in the city. These foundries produced the ornate cast ironwork that graced British and colonial towns, such as market halls, porticos, conservatories, bandstands, shop colonnades, shelters, drinking fountains, gates, lamp posts, railings and brackets. Macfarlane's was taken over by Allied Ironfounders in 1965 and demolished in 1967; it has been replaced by a modern industrial estate.

GOVAN A Glasgow trolleybus adds to the kaleidoscope of colour at Govan Cross on 2 June 1962 with gay bunting for Govan Fair; the red police and public telephone booths, and the gilded drinking fountain combining to brighten up this setting dominated by soot-stained, brown sandstone buildings. The Burgh of Govan was incorporated into the City of Glasgow in 1912.

The trolleybus is on route 106, which replaced tram line 7 from Bellahouston to Millerston in 1958. The trolleybuses on this route were themselves replaced by motorbuses in 1966 and the last trolleybuses ran through here on route 108 from Shieldhall to Mount Florida in 1967. The tram tracks and trolleybus wires in Govan were also used by Fairfield shipyard trains, with electric, steeple-cab locomotives, collecting steel, forgings and timber from Govan railway goods yard (off left), an operation that ceased in 1966.

The drinking fountain is a memorial to John Aitken, physician and surgeon, former Medical Officer to the Burgh, Govan Police and the collieries at Ibrox and Drumoyne. It has since been moved to the right and repainted crimson. The two telephone booths and the underground lavatories have gone. The British Linen Bank is now the Bank of Scotland and Govan railway goods yard is now the bus station. The shops and tenements on the left have been replaced by the redbrick, three-storey Govan Shopping Centre. Like Bridgeton Cross, Glasgow Cross and Anderston Cross, Govan Cross is now only a ghost of a once busy community centre.

GOVAN The original *Queen Mary* is seen steaming down the Clyde past Govan on a day excursion 'doon the watter' on 2 June 1962, watched by passengers and crew on the small Govan passenger ferry at its berth. On the right are some of the cranes of Harland & Wolff's seven-berth shipbuilding yard, which closed the following year. Astern of *Queen Mary* a cargo ship is berthed at Yorkhill Quay. The passenger ferry closed in 1966 and reopened in 2012. Merchant shipping retreated downriver to larger docks at Shieldhall and Greenock in the 1970s.

The *Queen Mary* was built by William Denny & Brothers at Dumbarton in 1932-33, and at 871 gross tons was the largest of Williamson Buchanan's famous fleet of fast, quiet and comfortable turbine steamers with two funnels and black and white paintwork. She was billed as 'Britain's finest pleasure steamer' and plied day trips from Glasgow Bridge Wharf to Dunoon, Rothesay and Largs. She was renamed *Queen Mary II* when the Cunard ocean liner *Queen Mary* was launched at Clydebank in 1935. The Williamson Buchanan fleet amalgamated with the LMSR's Caledonian Steam Packet Company in 1939. During the Hitler war *Queen Mary II* was painted grey and worked the Greenock-Dunoon ferry and tendered troopships in the firth, including the *Queen Mary*. In 1957 she was reboilered as an oil-burner with one funnel as seen here. After a refit in 1971 she went on the routes to Campbeltown and Inveraray.

The Caledonian and MacBrayne fleets amalgamated in 1973 and *Queen Mary II* had her original name restored in 1976 when the Cunarder

retired from service to Long Beach, California – but the Clyde queen had only one more year to run. When laid up she was sold to Glasgow District Council for a maritime museum that never materialised, and was then towed to Chatham for a cosmetic refit to restore her two-funnelled, black and white appearance. She then served as a floating restaurant at Savoy Pier, Westminster, from 1988 to 2009, before languishing in Tilbury docks. Friends of TS Queen Mary bought the ship in 2015 and had her towed back to Greenock in 2016 for preservation on the Clyde.

Right: **GOVAN** The vehicular ferry at Govan was one of the strangest craft afloat. Others of this design worked Finnieston ferry and Whiteinch ferry and there was one relief vessel, all operated by the Clyde Navigation Trust. In 1912 this elevating-deck ferry replaced the former chain ferry on the passage between Water Row, Govan, and Ferry Road, Pointhouse, and coped with the 14-foot tidal range by raising and lowering the vehicle deck to align it with the loading bays on each side of the river. They were double-ended vessels with twin screws at each end to save turning round in the busy, narrow fairway, and the wheelhouse was centrally situated on top of the central gantry. This vessel was No 4 in the fleet, built in 1937, 275 gross tons, 82 feet long and 44 feet wide. The ferry ran day and night carrying not only vehicles but also foot passengers working at the shipyards on both sides of the river here and the mills at Partick. This picture was taken from beside the Govan landing bay on 2 June 1962. On the opposite bank is Pointhouse, on the confluence of the rivers Clyde and Kelvin, site of the former shipyard of A. & J. Inglis, who built Britain's last three paddle steamers: *Lincoln Castle* (1941) and *Waverley* (1947) for the LNER and *Maid of the Loch* (1953) for BR. Both Govan ferries, vehicular and passenger, closed in 1966, two years after the opening of the second bore of the Clyde road tunnel a short way downriver. All the industrial buildings and cranes at Pointhouse have been cleared and this is now the parkland site of the spectacularly modern Riverside Museum of Transport, which saw the reopening of Govan passenger ferry in 2012.

Below: **GOVAN** The vast hulls of new ships under construction on the stocks of the Fairfield Shipbuilding & Engineering Company at Govan are seen on 2 June 1962. Govan was the centre of shipbuilding on the Clyde, starting with wooden ships in 1841. Fairfield was the name of the farm on the site of the shipyard opened in 1864 by Randolph, Elder & Company. John Elder was the marine engineer who invented the fuel-efficient compound steam engine, which allowed for longer voyages. The Fairfield company was founded in 1888 and this Govan yard grew to be the largest and busiest shipbuilding yard in Britain. In its heyday it employed more than 5,000 men building freighters, passenger liners and warships. Shipbuilding was heavy, noisy and dangerous work, carried out in the open in all weathers and there were many accidents with loss of limbs and life. British shipyards were still using 19th-century equipment and working practices after the Hitler war, there was a different trade union for almost every trade in the yard, and the industry was plagued by job demarcation, union disputes and late delivery, losing orders to competitive German, Swedish and Japanese shipyards, which had modernised equipment and methods after the war. The Fairfield company was bankrupt in 1966 but the yard kept going under receivers and a succession of new managements: Upper Clyde Shipbuilders (an amalgamation with four other yards), Lithgow's, the Norwegian firm Kvaerner, BVT Surface Fleet and now, since 2009, BAE Systems Surface Ships. This firm also owns the former Yarrow shipyard at Scotstoun and specialises in building ships for the Royal Navy. These are the only two shipyards left on the Clyde today and have been transformed with modern equipment and construction slips housed in huge sheds. They are allied to BAE Systems Submarine Solutions at Barrow.

Inverness-shire

Below: **AVIEMORE** Back to the 1890s: ex-Caledonian Railway 0-4-4 tank engine No 55173, dating from 1895, is seen by Aviemore signal cabin, built in 1898, on the former Highland Railway main line between Perth and Inverness, with the Cairngorm Mountains in the background, in August 1956. The engine is at rest while the crew takes a break on the trackside. Most of these engines were fitted with 'stovepipe' chimneys as seen here.

Above: **AVIEMORE** This 1929 Cowieson-bodied Albion motorbus was used as a motor caravan with a travelling fair when photographed alongside a 1936 Ford V8 car at Aviemore in August 1956. Both Albion and Cowieson were Glasgow firms and Scotland's leading bus-builders in their time. Albion produced the largest-capacity engines on the British bus market. The large steering wheel seems almost to fill the cab and the steering mechanism projects through the dash panel to the steering column projects through the dash panel to the steering mechanism on the front axle. The bus was new to Northern General Motors of Arbroath, which served the area between Dundee and Aberdeen. That company was taken over in 1930 by W. Alexander & Sons of Falkirk, serving much of central and eastern Scotland, and this bus was sold out of service in 1939 to Banff County Council and finally to Mr A. Dick, the showman, of Fochabers. Its top speed was about 20mph, which was the legal limit when it was new. In the background are the braes of the Monadh Liath ranged along the west side of Strathspey.

MALLAIG, the end of the road and the main fishing port on the west coast of Scotland, is noted for its herring and kippers. It occupies a rocky headland between the sea and a sheltered bay. This view across the harbour to the village of Courteachen on the other side of the bay was taken on 23 May 1959. Mallaig is at the end of the old 'Road to the Isles' that goes 'by Tummel and Loch Rannoch and Lochaber'. It is also the terminus of the scenic West Highland Extension Railway, 45 miles from Fort William, opened by the North British Railway in 1901, the last main-line extension in Britain, albeit single track, for services from Glasgow Queen Street. With the Grouping of railways in 1923 Mallaig became one of the remote western outposts – together with Seacombe, Silloth and Southport – of the LNER, which otherwise served the eastern side of Britain. From here one boards a ferry to 'the tangle of the isles' (Muck, Eigg, Rum and Canna) or 'over the sea to Skye', all of which boldly crown the horizon west and north of Mallaig. In 1959, when this picture was taken, the road from Fort William to Mallaig was still a tortuous, single-lane route with passing places, reminiscent of the old Khyber Pass, an adventure to drive along. Since then the road has been further blasted out, straightened and widened through the rocky landscape and rebuilt as a less arduous, two-lane carriageway, but it has lost its romance and sense of adventure. Fish from Mallaig now goes by road instead of by rail. The railway was dieselised in the 1960s but special steam trains run from Fort William in the summer holidays and the growth of tourism has altered the character of this workaday fishing port.

Index of locations

The Transport Travelogue series *(Volume numbers shown refer to the Recollections series numbering)*

Vol 70: A Transport Travelogue by road rail and water, 1948-1972
Part 1, South-east England: Kent, London and Sussex

July 2018	169 x 238mm	64pp	c60col/b&w	£8.00
ISBN: 978 1 85794 503 4	Softcover		By Cedric Greenwood	

Vol 71: A Transport Travelogue by road, rail and water, 1948-1972
Part 2, South and South West England: Wessex to Cornwall

July 2018	169 x 238mm	48pp	c60col/b&w	£6.00
ISBN: 978 1 85794 502 7	Softcover		By Cedric Greenwood	

Vol 72: A Transport Travelogue by road rail and water, 1948-1972
Part 3, Eastern and Midland Counties: Norfolk to Cheshire

July 2018	169 x 238mm	64pp	c60col/b&w	£8.00
ISBN: 978 1 85794 504 1	Softcover		By Cedric Greenwood	

Vol 73: A Transport Travelogue by road rail and water, 1948-1972
Part 4, Lancashire: Widnes to Furness

July 2018	169 x 238mm	64pp	c60col/b&w	£8.00
ISBN: 978 1 85794 499 0	Softcover		By Cedric Greenwood	

Vol 74: A Transport Travelogue by road rail and water, 1948-1972
Part 5, Yorkshire to the Border

July 2018	169 x 238mm	64pp	c60col/b&w	£8.00
ISBN: 978 1 85794 501 0	Softcover		By Cedric Greenwood	

Vol 94: A Transport Travelogue by road rail and water, 1948-1972
Part 6: Wales, Man and Scotland

July 2018	169 x 238mm	64pp	c60col/b&w	£8.00
ISBN: 978 1 85794 500 3	Softcover		By Cedric Greenwood	